39.-
HI

JUL - - 2016

POL POT'S

CAMBODIA

MATTHEW S. WELTIG

 TWENTY-FIRST CENTURY BOOKS   MINNEAPOLIS

Twenty-First Century Books
A division of Lerner Publishing Group, Inc.
241 First Avenue North
Minneapolis, MN 55401 U.S.A.

Website address: www.lernerbooks.com

Library of Congress Cataloging-in-Publication Data

Weltig, Matthew Scott.
    Pol Pot's Cambodia / by Matthew S. Weltig.
       p. cm. — (Dictatorships)
    Includes bibliographical references and index.
    ISBN 978–0–8225–8668–5 (lib. bdg. : alk. paper)
       1. Cambodia—History—1953–1975. 2. Cambodia--History--1975–1979.
    3. Political atrocities—Cambodia—History—20th century. 4. Pol Pot.
    I. Title.
    DS554.8.W46 2009
    959.604'2—dc22   2008000381

Manufactured in the United States of America
1 2 3 4 5 6 – DP – 14 13 12 11 10 09

CONTENTS

EVACUATION

APRIL 17, 1975. The people of Phnom Penh, the capital of Cambodia (a small Southeast Asian country), thought the war between government soldiers and Communist Khmer Rouge (Red Khmer) rebels had ended that morning. White flags flew from shops, houses, and government buildings. President Lon Nol had already fled. Crowds cheered the bedraggled Khmer Rouge soldiers as they marched down the streets.

Most of the people in the city welcomed the Khmer Rouge victory simply because it ended the war. Phnom Penh had become overcrowded with refugees from the countryside, where the war had been raging for eight years. Many of these refugees were living in unsanitary conditions, in a city teeming with disease and running out of food and supplies. Many residents were starving. Even those who opposed Communism, a political theory support-

OF PHNOM PENH

KHMER ROUGE SOLDIERS MARCH THROUGH THE STREETS OF PHNOM PENH,
Cambodia, on April 17, 1975, as city residents watch from the curbs.

ing revolution to redistribute wealth more fairly, thought peace would improve their lives.

But the Khmer Rouge victors' behavior was ominous. The soldiers, many of them young teenagers, had marched in elated in the morning, but they didn't celebrate their victory. They simply started searching for government officers. The Khmer Rouge soldiers knew that Cambodia's Communist revolution was just beginning.

The grim-faced soldiers in loose black uniforms also began ordering people to evacuate the city. Everyone had to leave, they said. Sometimes they gave a reason: with Phnom Penh in the hands of the Khmer Rouge, the anti-Communist United States was sure to bomb the city. (The United States had frequently bombed Cambodia during a long war that had recently ended against Communists in neighboring Vietnam.) Sometimes the soldiers said nothing. They just ordered people at gunpoint to leave immediately. When city residents asked where they should go, some soldiers told them to go to their home villages—even if their families had lived in Phnom Penh for generations. Others told people to wait in the city's outskirts or simply to go to the countryside.

Crowds milled through the streets and along the main highways, herded by Khmer Rouge soldiers. Babies wailed in their mothers' bony arms. The old and the ill hobbled along. Friends and relatives pushed hospital beds or carried the sick and injured on stretchers.

"Who ordered the evacuation?" some residents asked. When soldiers replied, their answer was cryptic. "Angkar," they said. "The Organization." Even the soldiers had only a vague idea of the Communist leadership that commanded them. And only the Communist Party's innermost circle knew who headed Angkar. It was Saloth Sar, a man who would become known to the world as Pol Pot. The masses streaming from Phnom Penh were embarking on one of the bloodiest social experiments in history—Pol Pot's Cambodia.

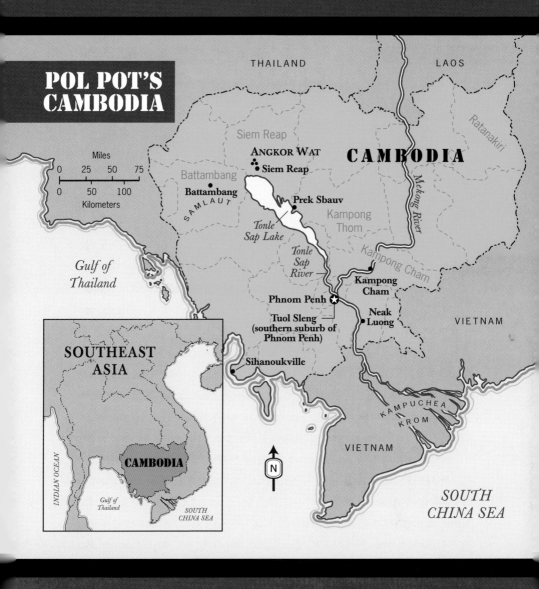

POL POT'S CAMBODIA

THAILAND

LAOS

Ratanakiri

Miles
0   25   50   75
0   50   100
Kilometers

Siem Reap

ANGKOR WAT
Siem Reap

CAMBODIA

Battambang
Battambang

SAMLAUT

Prek Sbauv

Tonle
Sap Lake

Kampong
Thom

Gulf of
Thailand

Tonle
Sap
River

Kampong Cham

Kampong
Cham

Phnom Penh

Tuol Sleng
(southern suburb of
Phnom Penh)

Neak
Luong

VIETNAM

SOUTHEAST
ASIA

Sihanoukville

CAMBODIA

INDIAN OCEAN

Gulf of
Thailand

SOUTH
CHINA SEA

KAMPUCHEA
KROM

VIETNAM

N

SOUTH
CHINA SEA

CHAPTER 1

THE MAKING

MANY POLITICAL TRENDS AND EVENTS led to the 1975 Khmer Rouge takeover that put Saloth Sar in command of Cambodia. Most of these happened during Sar's lifetime. Nationalism, the idea that Cambodia should be independent of French rule, grew popular in the 1930s while Sar was a young student in Phnom Penh. Cambodia felt the effects of World War II (1939–1945) as Sar finished his studies in the capital and moved to the Cambodian city of Kampong Cham for high school. In the 1940s and 1950s, as Sar's education continued in Cambodia and France, Communist revolutions were under way in nearby China and Vietnam. The Cold War (1945–1991) between the United States and the Soviet Union, with U.S. opposition to the global spread of Communism, also influenced events in Cambodia. This was especially true when U.S. involvement in the war between Vietnam's Communist and non-Communist forces spilled over into

ROF A
REVOLUTIONARY

Cambodia in the late 1960s and 1970s. And throughout Sar's life, various events inflamed many Cambodians' distrust and resentment toward Vietnam, Cambodia's ancient rival.

THE CAMBODIA OF
YOUNG SALOTH SAR

Saloth Sar was born on May 19, 1928—or perhaps 1925. (Sar's account of his life often differs from others' accounts.) His family lived in Prek Sbauv, a village in Kampong Thom Province in north central Cambodia. He had six older brothers and sisters. Like most

Cambodians, his family was of the Khmer ethnic group. (Many other ethnic groups, such as Vietnamese, Thai, Lao, Chinese, Cham, and those of various hill tribes, also lived in Cambodia at that time.)

The Saloth family were farmers, like most Cambodians. But they weren't poor. They worked 30 acres (12 hectares) of land, tending rice and other crops with several oxen. They grew enough food to sell the surplus and make a comfortable income. They lived in one

COMMUNISM

Communism, or Marxism-Leninism, is a theory developed in the nineteenth century by German philosophers Karl Marx and Friedrich Engels. In the twentieth century, Russian leader Vladimir Lenin refined and put it into practice through the revolution that led to the creation of the Communist Soviet Union in 1922.

The theory states that struggles between social classes dominate history. A key struggle is between workers and those who exploit them in feudal or capitalist societies. In a feudal society, the nobility and royalty exploit peasants by requiring them to give up the products of their labor for nothing in return. In a capitalist society, capitalists pay workers for their labor, but the capitalists own the raw materials, the tools and factories needed to make products, and the end products themselves. Therefore, it is the capitalists, not the workers, who profit from the workers' labor. The workers cannot even set the price of their own labor, as the market determines the price of wages—just as it does any other commodity, such as gold or sugar.

Among other things, Communists believe in armed revolution to of Prek Sbauv's largest houses. They even had some connections to Cambodia's royal family in Phnom Penh, which opened up job and schooling opportunities.

In the 1920s, a king still ruled Cambodia. Cambodia was, in fact, an ancient kingdom. Its people looked back with pride on the Angkor period (800s–1400s) as the pinnacle of their civilization. During this time, Cambodians built massive irrigation works and

empower the oppressed classes (mainly workers and peasants) and to create a more equitable society. In this new society, the workers themselves would own the means of production, including the land for farming and the factories for producing finished goods as well as their own labor power. The society would distribute the products of labor to the laborers themselves rather than to capitalists or nobles. In practice, this means that the government would control the means of production and distribute finished products. Private ownership of property would be abolished. (In Communist theory, private ownership would lead to some individuals storing up wealth, which they could use as capital, while others would have to rely on selling their labor to survive. Private property would thus lead to exploitation of workers, in a return to capitalism.)

Because it offered hope to oppressed peoples, Communism became a very successful international movement. In fact, in the years after World War II, the Soviet Union emerged as one of the world's superpowers, and much of twentieth-century global politics was driven by the Cold War—the struggle for dominance between the Soviet Union and the anti-Communist United States.

KING SURYAVARMAN II BUILT ANGKOR WAT IN THE EARLY 1100S. THE HUGE
temple complex in northern Cambodia also served as the capital city of his kingdom.

canals to boost rice production and to ease travel and shipping. A long association with Indian merchants and religious leaders had led to the introduction of the Hindu religion and practices associated with Hinduism, such as giving kings divine (godlike) status. The Angkor period also produced the magnificent temple complex of Angkor Wat, for worship of the Hindu god Vishnu.

But the Angkor period did not last forever. Greedy god-kings bankrupted the kingdom with extravagant construction projects. And absolute power was so tempting that princes gladly conspired with neighboring Thai or Vietnamese monarchs against rival claimants to the throne. For hundreds of years after the Angkor period, Thailand and Vietnam alternately dominated Cambodia, claiming territory as their own. In periods when it was independent, Cambodia had to carefully balance its neighbors' support. Over time, Cambodians abandoned Angkor as the political capital. Only the temple complex, where a group of Buddhist monks lived, remained continuously inhabited. Phnom Penh, which lies at the confluence (meeting point) of the Mekong and the Tonle Sap rivers, became the new capital.

By the early 1860s, Thailand and Vietnam had claimed authority over all Cambodia. In an effort to preserve his throne and Cambodian independence from those two countries, Cambodia's King Norodom agreed to make the country a French protectorate in 1863. Under this arrangement, France would protect Norodom and Cambodia from Thailand and Vietnam, but Norodom would give up his foreign policy decisions to France.

As the years went by, French influence grew. By the 1880s, the French were imposing ever-increasing taxes. The French used some of this money to modernize Phnom Penh and support Cambodia's traditional Buddhist schools but spent most of it elsewhere in their empire. They introduced some public works projects in Cambodia, such as building roads throughout the kingdom, but these relied on unpaid Cambodian labor. France brought over bureaucrats from its preferred colony, Vietnam, rather than educating and choosing Cambodian officials to rule the protectorate. Over time, a French-speaking elite developed in the cities.

On the other hand, France made no effort to turn Cambodia into a completely French-speaking, French-cultured colony. The French encouraged study of Buddhism, which had become the main religion of Cambodia by the fourteenth century. French scholars focused on the glories of the Angkor period. In the early 1900s, the French even convinced Thailand and Vietnam to return large pieces of Cambodian territory. The returned territories included Angkor Wat, which French scholars helped restore. Not only the

French but also Cambodians came to see the temple complex as the primary symbol of Cambodia.

The French presence was a mixed blessing. As taxation increased and French control tightened, Cambodians occasionally protested. Demonstrations were sometimes massive. One even resulted in the death of a French tax collector. But besides opposing taxes, Cambodians seemed ambivalent toward the French throughout the 1920s. Raising crops, catching fish, avoiding bandits, and other local issues were uppermost in Cambodians' minds.

SALOTH SAR'S SCHOOLING

Around 1934 Saloth Sar's family sent him to a Buddhist monastery in Phnom Penh for religious training. Two years later, he began attending the Miche School, a Catholic school in the city. He studied there for the next six years. During this time, he lived with three of his older brothers, who were already in Phnom Penh. To hide his privileges and exaggerate his peasant background, Sar later claimed, "I am from a peasant family, during my childhood, I lived with my parents and helped them in their agricultural works." His first official biography, broadcast on North Korean radio, said he'd learned to read and write during six years at pagoda school (a traditional school run by Buddhist monks) and that he "engaged in farming with his parents from 1937 to 1939."

Living in Phnom Penh provided Sar with a new view of the status of the Khmer people. Unlike in his home village, in 1930s Phnom Penh, Khmer residents formed a minority of the population. Merchants were generally Chinese. Most government workers were Vietnamese. Some French officials lived in Phnom Penh. The city also included a Cham quarter. Each ethnic group had a separate community within the capital.

Important social changes were happening in Phnom Penh in the 1930s. The French began to spend more money on education in Cambodia. Because of this, a new Cambodian elite educated at French high schools began to arise in Phnom Penh. The alumni organization of one French-founded institution, the Sisowath School, grew in numbers and influence. In 1930 a Frenchwoman named Suzanne Karpelés founded another important organization, the Buddhist Institute. This institute's focus on Cambodia's glorious past attracted Cambodia's intellectuals as well as its Buddhist priests.

Another new institution—the first Khmer-language newspaper, *Nagaravatta* (Angkor Wat)—had close ties with the Buddhist Institute. The strongly nationalist newspaper debuted in 1936. It opposed Vietnamese control of the Cambodian administration and Chinese control of Cambodian trade and financial transactions, and its articles frequently voiced anti-Vietnamese sentiments. It didn't call directly for action against the French, but it became an important mouthpiece for Cambodian independence.

A man named Son Ngoc Thanh linked these three organizations. He was born in Kampuchea Krom (lower Cambodia), the Mekong Delta region of Vietnam. A large group of Khmer people had lived there at least since the Angkor period, when Cambodia occupied the area, and possibly centuries longer. Son Ngoc Thanh studied first at pagoda school, then at university and law school in France. After leaving France in the 1930s, he worked in Cambodia as a judge and a public prosecutor. Then he took an important position at the Buddhist Institute. He joined *Nagaravatta* soon after it was founded, and he also became legal counsel for the Sisowath alumni group. Through his influence, the alumni group began to send Buddhist monks around the country to preach against French control of Cambodia. Son Ngoc Thanh soon became a leader of the Cambodian independence movement.

WORLD WAR II

In the late 1930s, the Cambodian elite in Phnom Penh continued to grow and promote Cambodian independence. Saloth Sar studied and formed friendships with other Khmer students. And World War II began. This war—with theaters of battle all over the world, including Asia—invigorated Cambodia's nationalists. It also indirectly split them into Communist and non-Communist factions (groups).

At the onset of World War II, the Axis powers (Germany, Japan, and Italy) invaded neighboring countries. France surrendered to Germany in the summer of 1940. Soon thereafter, Son Ngoc Thanh approached the French resident superior in Phnom Penh and asked France to grant Cambodia's independence. He reasoned that a conquered France could no longer protect Cambodia. But France refused to give up control. As Japanese troops entered Indochina (the Asian peninsula between India and China), *Nagaravatta* loudly criticized French rule.

At the same time, Thailand saw France's defeat by the Germans as a chance to regain Cambodian territory it had given to the French. Thai troops therefore invaded Cambodia by land and defeated the French throughout Battambang and Siem Reap provinces—except one French garrison protecting the Angkor Wat temple complex. Though the Thai invasion largely succeeded on land, the French navy defeated the Thai fleet at sea in January 1941. Japan demanded that the two sides negotiate a settlement. In a Japanese-mediated agreement, Battambang and most of Siem Reap reverted to Thailand. The French kept the Angkor Wat complex. To Cambodian nationalists, Thanh's predictions had come true: a weakened France had failed to protect Cambodia.

In May 1941, Japanese troops marched on Phnom Penh. Japan was conquering much of eastern and Southeast Asia, and it proclaimed an end to European colonies throughout the region. However, the conquest of Cambodia was largely for show. Japan had already come to an agreement with Cambodia's French officials. A new government called the Vichy regime had come to power in France, and it was friendly with Japan's ally Germany. The Vichy government ordered the French in Cambodia not to oppose Japan. Many Cambodian nationalists, such as Son Ngoc Thanh, welcomed the Japanese as liberators. For this reason, the token Japanese invasion of Cambodia met little opposition. Japan preserved the French administration and installed only a small garrison of Japanese soldiers. Japan did not take over the Cambodian government.

Still in control but threatened by Cambodian nationalism, the French tried to strengthen their position. In 1942 they closed down *Nagaravatta* for its anti-French stance. They replaced the nation's traditional Buddhist lunar calendar with the Gregorian calendar used throughout Europe. They also planned a switch from the forty-seven–letter Khmer alphabet to the twenty-six–letter Latin alphabet of western European languages such as French. These changes upset the monks associated with the Buddhist Institute. Son Ngoc Thanh decided that the time for action had come. With the approval of some Japanese officers, he began to plan a coup (overthrow) that would replace the French with a pro-Japanese Cambodian government.

The French then took a step that enraged Cambodian Buddhists. In July 1942, French police arrested two monks for asking Khmer soldiers in the French army to desert. One of these monks was an important, widely respected professor. The arrest violated Buddhist custom, which held that nonreligious authorities could not arrest monks. Traditionally, if a monk were accused of a crime, the police would wait for his fellow monks to remove him from his position. Then the police would arrest him. In this case, the French seized and imprisoned the two monks without consulting other monks. This insult inflamed anti-French feelings.

Son Ngoc Thanh saw in this widespread anger an opportunity to stake a claim for nationalism. The time for action had come. With a *Nagaravatta* associate, he organized a massive demonstration. One to two thousand people, including about five hundred monks, gathered behind the royal palace in Phnom Penh to protest. The crowd demanded release of the imprisoned monks, a new constitution, and a pro-Japanese Cambodian government.

When French authorities refused to admit protesters to the French resident superior's office building, a riot began. The French police clubbed the protesters with batons. The protesters—monks included—fought back with rocks and sticks. Two trucks of Japanese soldiers arrived, but they just looked on. Although many people were injured, none died. Over the next two days, the French arrested about two hundred people. Many protesters fled to the countryside and to neighboring Thailand and Vietnam. Son Ngoc Thanh eventually made his way to Japan.

The French sent the arrested nationalists to prison in Vietnam. There they met Vietnamese prisoners who had been arrested for supporting the Viet Minh, a Vietnamese independence group. The Cambodians found much in common with the Viet Minh and began

PSEUDONYMS

To protect the secrecy of their movement, Communists in non-Communist countries often used pseudonyms. Communist leaders also sometimes took names that had special meanings. For example, Son Ngoc Minh combined the names of his role models (Son Ngoc Thanh and Ho Chi Minh). And Ho Chi Minh's name means "the enlightened one." Saloth Sar's best-known pseudonym, Pol Pot, has no particular meaning. But because it sounds like a common Khmer peasant name, it disguises Saloth Sar's somewhat privileged background.

to learn from them. Many Viet Minh were Communists, and many of the imprisoned Cambodians began to embrace Communism too.

The Cambodian Issarak (independence) movement had begun to split into two factions. One was centered in western Cambodia and in Thailand. These Issaraks considered Son Ngoc Thanh their leader. They received some support from Thailand. Communists dominated the other Issarak faction, centered in eastern Cambodia and in Vietnam. Although their differing ideologies (political worldviews and goals) occasionally led to clashes between non-Communist Issaraks and the Viet Minh, the two factions were not yet entirely at odds with each other. In fact, one monk who fled arrest after the Phnom Penh demonstration took the pseudonym (false name) Son Ngoc Minh, which combined the names of Son Ngoc Thanh and Vietnamese Communist leader Ho Chi Minh. Son Ngoc Minh became an important Cambodian Communist revolutionary in Vietnam.

During the turbulent year of 1942, Saloth Sar left Phnom Penh. He had hoped to attend high school in the city, but he failed the entrance exams. Instead, he went to the market town of Kampong Cham to attend the Norodom Sihanouk High School. There he studied during the rest of World War II.

KING NORODOM SIHANOUK

The end of World War II brought changes in Cambodia's government that strongly influenced both types of Issarak movement. Cambodia's new young king, Norodom Sihanouk, became a key political figure in the postwar years.

Norodom Sihanouk had become king in April 1941 after the death of his grandfather, Sisowath Monivong. French authorities chose this eighteen-year-old prince instead of the king's son, Sisowath Monireth. They claimed that crowning Norodom Sihanouk would ease tensions within the royal family. They probably also thought the younger man would be easier to control. He was then a high school student in Vietnam, and he seemed to care more about movies and ice cream than about politics.

In 1945, a few years into the new king's reign, World War II was not going well for the Axis powers. In Europe, France had already been freed from German control and the Vichy government removed. In Southeast Asia, Japan expected new French opposition to Japanese rule. It also thought French officials would help the Allies (countries fighting against Japan, Germany, and Italy in World War II) as they intensified their fight against Japan. So Japan decided to remove French officials from power all over Indochina and replace them with local governments. The French officials raised little resistance when Japan removed them on March 9, 1945. On March 13,

KAMPUCHEA

The term *Kampuchea* comes from a word in the ancient Indian language of Sanskrit. It refers to a group of Indian people believed by some to be the ancestors of the Cambodian people. To demonstrate Cambodian independence, some Cambodian regimes have insisted on this spelling of the nation's name (which best approximates the pronunciation in Khmer, Cambodia's official language) rather than the French spelling (*Cambodge*) or the English one (*Cambodia*).

urged to do so by the Japanese, Norodom Sihanouk announced the independence of the Kingdom of Kampuchea.

The king made some changes that pleased Cambodia's nationalists. The nation reinstated its Buddhist calendar and Khmer writing system. The people of Phnom Penh celebrated the 1942 demonstration leaders as heroes. Son Ngoc Thanh returned from Japan, and Norodom Sihanouk made him foreign minister.

However, the king filled the rest of his cabinet with members of the pro-French elite. This upset nationalists. In August 1945, a coup supported by monks and Sisowath alumni removed most of the cabinet ministers. Son Ngoc Thanh soon rose to the position of prime minister.

This period of independence was very short-lived. When World War II ended with Japan's surrender in September 1945, the Allies swept through Indochina removing Japanese forces. The French returned to Cambodia and prepared to reinstate their government. French officials arrested Son Ngoc Thanh in October 1945.

Rather than try to maintain complete independence, Norodom

Sihanouk preferred to compromise with the French. He felt this would help him control the nationalists who had taken over his cabinet in August. Cambodia remained independent in name but became a member of the French Union. The king allowed a return of French authority over Cambodian foreign affairs and over many of the nation's internal matters.

Although nationalist leader Son Ngoc Thanh was in prison and the French had returned to power, Cambodian nationalism remained alive. In the northwest, a group called Khmer Issarak took up arms against the French. In August 1946, it managed to occupy the Angkor Wat temples for several days. Thailand supported Khmer Issarak because it worked in Battambang and Siem Reap provinces, which Thailand still controlled, to oppose the return of French officials. In November 1946, Thailand ceded Battambang and Siem Reap to Cambodia as a condition for joining the United Nations (a newly created international organization working for world peace). However, Thailand kept supporting Khmer Issarak, who continued their guerrilla activities against the French. (Guerrilla activities involve a military group fighting against formal government troops, typically using harassment, sabotage, and terror.)

Meanwhile, events in Vietnam continued to influence the independence movement in southeastern Cambodia. Ho Chi Minh had declared Vietnam's independence from France as Japan withdrew at the end of World War II. As France tried to reassert control, the First Indochina War (1946–1954) began between France and Vietnamese independence forces. Many Cambodian nationalists who were already in Vietnam or eastern Cambodia saw their independence tied to Vietnam's. They fought the French in Vietnam and learned both military tactics and Communist ideology there. They brought both their ideology and their guerrilla warfare tactics to the countryside of eastern Cambodia. There they fought, sometimes in conjunction with non-Communist Issarak groups, for Cambodian independence.

Cambodian nationalism wasn't confined to the border regions. Norodom Sihanouk's policies allowed nationalists to develop a political arm in Phnom Penh too. In 1946 the king and French officials drew up a new constitution. The king insisted that an elected national assembly should approve the constitution. All male Cambodians should have a right to vote for assembly members. The French agreed to this plan. Three political parties arose to compete for assembly seats. One party, the Democrats, had support from *Nagaravatta*, the Sisowath alumni, and many monks. It also gained wide support among the people, for most of its local candidates were popular Buddhist monks.

KING NORODOM SIHANOUK *(CENTER)* REVIEWS TROOPS AT HIS PHNOM PENH palace in 1947.

SALOTH SAR'S HIGHER EDUCATION

Involvement with the Democrats strongly influenced the course of Saloth Sar's life. The Democrats attracted many students, including Saloth Sar, to their cause. These students formed strong friendships, gained new political ideas, and formed connections with powerful politicians as they worked on the Democrats' 1947 election campaign.

Sar wasn't a star student, but he was diligent. After finishing high school, he returned to Phnom Penh to study carpentry at a technical school. He impressed those who met him during this period, but he didn't yet demonstrate strong political ambition or skill. Although he did some work for the Democrats, he seemed more interested in school and sports.

Several of Saloth Sar's high school classmates from Kampong Cham, including Khieu Samphan, Hu Nim, and Hou Youn, also went to Phnom Penh. They attended the more elite Sisowath School. There they met the intelligent Ieng Sary, a student from Kampuchea Krom. Passionate about politics, Sary founded a student nationalist group at the Sisowath School. He also became deeply involved with the Democrats.

Saloth Sar and Ieng Sary became close friends in 1947 as they worked for the Democrats' campaign. The campaign succeeded. Democrats won fifty of the sixty-seven assembly seats. However, the party soon became plagued with external and internal problems. The countryside was growing unstable due to anti-French guerrilla activities carried out by the Khmer Issarak and the Viet Minh's Cambodian allies. This unrest often prevented the government from collecting taxes, and Cambodia began to have financial difficulty. Problems also occurred within the government. Although the Democrats were known for fighting corruption, several scandals involving important Democrats happened while the party held power. This allowed non-Democrats to replace Democrats in key cabinet positions (seats on the king's advisory council). The government was soon deadlocked. In September 1949, Norodom Sihanouk dissolved the assembly, which he saw as an obstacle to a government that would do his bidding. He postponed elections indefinitely, leaving the country governed by a cabinet of his choosing.

Ieng Sary led a student strike to protest the king's actions. Then, with the Democrats' efforts stymied by the king's new cabinet, he applied for—and won—a scholarship to study at the elite Paris Institute of Political Studies. Saloth Sar also won a scholarship to study in Paris, at the French School of Radio-Electricity.

Saloth Sar arrived in France in September 1949. It was here that he became deeply political and cemented the connections that guided his and Cambodia's future. In 1950 Sar joined a quasi-Communist group called the Marxist Circle. Ieng Sary and some other Cambodian students led the circle. Its members included Khieu Samphan and Hou Youn.

In 1950s Paris, Communism was popular among idealistic intellectuals. They hoped to improve the world and spread economic equality. Communism—which promotes broad social and economic equality—seemed full of promise. The Communist-led Soviet Union had emerged as a world superpower, and other Communist revolutions were under way too. The world's other emerging superpower, the United States, seemed arrogant and self-serving, supporting unpopular puppet governments in various nations at the expense of the people's good.

China, a major power in eastern Asia, was one of the nations undergoing a Communist revolution as Saloth Sar began his studies in Paris. Cambodian students in Paris were hearing reports of a similar revolution in their own country. Although Saloth Sar and the other Cambodians knew few details, many felt their country was riding a historic wave of change that would lead to a Communist utopia (perfect society).

Saloth Sar had a formative experience in the summer of 1950. During summer vacation, lacking money and curious about life in a Communist country, he went to the southeastern European nation of Yugoslavia to join a work brigade. He accompanied a group of Cambodian and French students who volunteered to carry out public works projects there. At that time, Yugoslavia was an independent Communist country. Although governed by its Communist party, Yugoslavia refused to let the powerful Soviet Union dictate its policies. In the Cold War, Yugoslavia sided with neither the United States nor the Soviet Union. While in Yugoslavia, Saloth Sar saw for the first time a small Communist country's attempts to collectivize agriculture (reorganize it into publicly owned communal farms).

In 1951, two of Cambodia's female intellectuals, Khieu Thirith and her older sister Khieu Ponnary, arrived in Paris. Both sisters were among the first women to study at the Sisowath School, and Khieu Ponnary was the first Cambodian woman to receive a baccalaureate (bachelor's) degree. Ieng Sary and Khieu Thirith married soon thereafter, and Khieu Thirith changed her name to Ieng Thirith. Khieu Ponnary would eventually marry Saloth Sar.

Saloth Sar and Ieng Sary continued to attend the Marxist Circle. While not exactly a Communist organization, it was a reading club where young Khmer students gathered to discuss Communist and leftist texts. (Leftists, or liberals, are people who support broad societal changes to improve the lives of the common people.) The Communist Party, on the other hand, was rigidly organized, exclusive, and often secretive. To become a member, a person needed a sponsor within the party and had to spend time as a candidate to prove party loyalty. Before acceptance into the party, a person might not know who its members were. Sar overcame these hurdles and became a member of the French Communist Party during his stay in Paris.

Acquaintances from Saloth Sar's Paris days recalled that he was intelligent and studious but ordinary. He seemed no different from any other Cambodian student. He was friendly and loved the cinema. He was so gentle that "he would not have killed a chicken." Although he was studious, the books he read were not his textbooks. He spent much of his time poring over political texts and French literature. This left him little time for his schoolwork, and he failed his classes three years in a row. When he lost his scholarship in 1952, he had to return to Cambodia.

Even good students in the Marxist Circle were losing their scholarships—for political reasons. Norodom Sihanouk and conservatives in the Cambodian government had noticed that Parisian education was converting many young Cambodians into Communists who opposed royalty. (Conservatives, or rightists, are people opposed to broad changes in society and to restricting free-market economic systems.)

Forced return to Cambodia was no great loss to Saloth Sar. He had decided to devote his life to effecting a Communist revolution. He wanted to go to the Cambodian countryside and find out what was really happening. Despite the value of his experience in Paris, France was still an imperialist power (a nation that controls other nations). Sar knew the time had come to go home and join the fight against France and Cambodia's monarchy.

THE EARLY 1950S

While Saloth Sar was studying Communism in Paris, various groups in Cambodia continued fighting for independence. These groups had nationalism in common, but their motives were quite different.

In the early 1950s, traditional attitudes were still strong among Cambodians, especially in rural areas. These people revered the king and considered his power absolute. So Norodom Sihanouk could count on firm support from the common people. Traditionalists also tended to be religious and to respect Buddhist monks. Traditionalist Issaraks saw themselves fighting against the French for Cambodian traditions—not against the old power structure.

At the same time, the Communist Viet Minh were supporting part of Cambodia's independence movement. So Communism continued to influence many nationalists. Communism opposed all forms of royalty and religion. Communists didn't profess this openly when recruiting supporters. In truth, though, they were fighting not only for independence but also for a dramatic change in Cambodian society.

Attitudes toward the Vietnamese also complicated Cambodian nationalism. Many Khmer people saw the Vietnamese as enemies. Vietnam was an ancient foe, and Vietnamese bureaucrats had dominated French Cambodia for decades. Vietnamese involvement in Cambodia's independence movement made some Cambodians worry that Vietnam would take over once the French were gone.

To further complicate matters, a new government had come to power in Thailand in the late 1940s. Khmer Issarak lost Thailand's support, and the group splintered. Some members refused to join the freedom fighters in eastern Cambodia because of the easterners' Communist connections. Others refused because of Vietnamese connections. In 1950 Vietnamese members and leaders dominated the Indochinese Communist Party (ICP).

The ICP tried to unite Cambodia's nationalists by forming the Khmer Issarak Association (KIA). Cambodian ICP members, including former monks Tou Samouth and Son Ngoc Minh, led the KIA. In 1951 the KIA proclaimed a new Cambodian government, with Son Ngoc Minh as president. This government exercised some authority over the one-third of Cambodia controlled at that time by the different Issarak movements. It claimed to be the rightful government of independent Cambodia, as opposed to the French-supported government in Phnom Penh.

The Communists also tried to change Cambodians' perception that Communism was a Vietnamese institution. In 1951 Cambodian Communists formed the Khmer People's Revolutionary Party (KPRP), a Communist Party separate from the ICP. The Vietnamese still controlled this party behind the scenes. But with Cambodian leaders—including former Buddhist monks—the KPRP could attract more Khmer Issaraks.

Meanwhile, in Phnom Penh, Norodom Sihanouk finally agreed to hold a 1951 election for a new national assembly. The Phnom Penh government could collect votes only in areas not controlled by guerrilla forces. Nevertheless, the election was fairly peaceful. Again, the Democrats won a majority of assembly seats.

To boost his popularity, the king convinced the French to release Son Ngoc Thanh from prison. Soon after the election, Son Ngoc Thanh returned to Phnom Penh, where the people welcomed him as a national hero. This made the king jealous and the French suspicious. Several months after his return, Son Ngoc Thanh disappeared in the jungle to join the non-Communist Issaraks. This move confirmed to Sihanouk and French officials that Thanh was a traitor to them. And the Democrats raised no outcry over Thanh's move, which deepened Sihanouk's suspicions about them. Thanh's move reinvigorated the non-Communist Issarak movement and attracted Thai support for it. But this move also drove a wedge between the Communist and non-Communist groups.

Around Cambodia and in France, student protesters demanded Cambodian independence and opposed Sihanouk, who continued to cooperate with the French. Many youths left Phnom Penh to join Son Ngoc Thanh. Norodom Sihanouk blamed the Democrats for these troubles. Supported by French troops, he dissolved the assembly and cabinet and formed a new cabinet of handpicked members.

In 1952 and 1953, Norodom Sihanouk strengthened his position and honed his style. He established himself as an absolute ruler, in the mold of the kings of the Angkor period. He ruthlessly pursued his opponents, arresting a number of the Democrats' leaders for conspiracy against the state. He also promised progress on popular causes, such as ending government corruption and French rule. He spent most of 1953 out of Cambodia, petitioning for independence.

CAMBODIANS WAIT TO MEET WITH King Norodom Sihanouk in 1952. The king hoped such meetings would increase his popularity with his subjects.

SALOTH SAR JOINS THE CAMBODIAN UNDERGROUND

Shortly before the king left for France, Saloth Sar arrived in Phnom Penh. He stayed in the capital for just a few months before setting out to gain some real revolutionary experience. His brother Saloth Chhay had joined Son Ngoc Thanh's forces, which sometimes worked with the Communists against the French. Saloth Chhay had been to the KIA's eastern headquarters several times. Saloth Sar used his brother's connections to get introduced to the KIA. With his credentials as a member of the French Communist Party, he also managed to join the ICP.

As an ICP member working for the KIA, Saloth Sar learned much from the Viet Minh. However, he chafed at the manual labor foisted on him: working in the kitchen and hauling waste from the lavatories. He may also have resented assignment to a cell (group) composed equally of Khmer and Vietnamese members, with the Vietnamese in the higher positions. But his dedication to Communism never wavered. He applied himself to learning all the Viet Minh could teach him. Under their tutelage, he began learning how to recruit peasants one by one and how to build up an underground (secret) organization during a guerrilla war.

Despite the divisions among Cambodia's fighters for independence, they were gaining ground. By 1953 French officials considered most of Cambodia unsafe. A large percentage of Cambodians lived in rebel-controlled areas, even though the government had tried to relocate them to areas that the government still controlled.

Norodom Sihanouk's independence negotiations made little progress at first. Frustrated at France's rejection, he traveled to Canada, the United States, and Japan. The United States gave him no official support, but he did strike upon a useful tactic there. He claimed that if Cambodia didn't gain independence soon, its people might join the Communist Viet Minh, the enemies of France and the United States.

This strategy was useful because the United States saw the ongoing war in Vietnam as necessary to stop the spread of Communism. Since 1950, in the wake of China's Communist revolution, the United States had been giving France military aid for the war in Vietnam. The United States feared that if Communists won in Vietnam, other countries in Asia would soon become Communist too.

Playing on French and U.S. fears got Norodom Sihanouk some attention, but gaining Cambodian independence required action, not just words. When the king returned to Cambodia in May 1953, he took about 30,000 troops and police with him to a new headquarters near Angkor. By August more than 130,000 people around the country had joined his cause. He asked France to arm these people against the Viet Minh, but France refused. The king began to call even more loudly for independence.

With this new pressure from the king and his supporters, granting independence to Cambodia seemed France's best course of action. If France armed Norodom Sihanouk's group without granting independence, it risked becoming the target of those weapons. If it didn't arm the group, Cambodia seemed likely to fall to the Viet Minh. In the end, France granted Cambodia independence on November 9, 1953. France did this in hopes that if Cambodia were independent, nationalists would no longer be drawn to the Communist movement.

The king portrayed himself as a liberator who had succeeded where both Son Ngoc Thanh and the Communists had failed. And his achievement did deflate the rebellion somewhat. Many members of the non-Communist Issarak groups had joined Norodom Sihanouk's campaign, abandoning the underground independence movement. Even some groups more closely aligned with Communists saw no reason to continue their activities.

However, not everyone abandoned the underground. The KIA and Viet Minh kept fighting. They claimed that Cambodia wasn't independent as long as French troops remained—which they did, until March 1954. Furthermore, the Communists who dominated the KIA wanted not only independence but also a social and governmental revolution. They claimed Norodom Sihanouk was a U.S. puppet. They believed it wasn't yet time to lay down arms. In 1954 the KPRP was two thousand members strong. The KIA fielded about five thousand Cambodian soldiers, who fought alongside about three thousand Viet Minh.

THE GENEVA CONFERENCE

In 1954 an international conference in Geneva, Switzerland, produced decisions that profoundly affected Cambodia. The conference's purpose was ending several wars between Communist and non-Communist forces in Asia. Representatives from the war-torn countries attended, as did diplomats from the United Kingdom, France, the United States, the Soviet Union, and China.

Before the conference took up the question of Indochina, the Viet Minh scored a major military victory over French forces at the battle at Dien Bien Phu in Vietnam. This victory gave Vietnam's Communists more leverage (power) in international negotiations. A cease-fire agreement divided Vietnam into two parts. French forces had to withdraw to South Vietnam; and the Viet Minh, to North Vietnam. Representatives from both North and South Vietnam could officially attend the Geneva negotiations. But only representatives from Norodom Sihanouk's government could speak for Cambodia. KIA members attended the conference as a part of the Viet Minh delegation, but they weren't allowed to represent Cambodia. As a result, the Geneva negotiations allowed Communists in Vietnam to maintain a fairly strong position but weakened Communists in Cambodia.

Another reason the Geneva Conference weakened Cambodian Communists was a decision among the Communist nations to concentrate on helping the Communists win in Vietnam. A successful Communist revolution in Cambodia seemed unlikely. But the Viet Minh dominated North Vietnam and also had much support in South Vietnam. Dividing Vietnam—with Communists in control of the north and the south's fate to be determined by a later election—seemed favorable to Communist leaders at the conference. However, this decision required the Viet Minh in Cambodia to withdraw to North Vietnam. The conference didn't allocate any of Cambodia's Communist-controlled territory to an independent Cambodian Communist authority.

DELEGATES FROM THE SOVIET UNION, THE UNITED KINGDOM, LAOS, FRANCE, Vietnam, Cambodia, and the United States meet at the Geneva Conference in 1954.

POL POT'S CAMBODIA

After the Geneva Conference, Cambodian Communists felt betrayed by the international Communist movement—especially by Vietnamese Communists. This feeling contributed to the anti-Vietnamese nature Cambodia's Communist revolution eventually developed.

The Geneva Conference had other consequences for Cambodia too. It formally recognized Cambodian independence and Norodom Sihanouk's government and called for national assembly elections in 1955. The United States began to supply the king with military and economic aid to fend off the threat of Vietnamese Communism spreading throughout Cambodia. Since the KIA's government went unrecognized by the international community, this made the armed Communist rebels illegal.

THE 1955 ELECTIONS

Communist rebels in Cambodia faced a choice: join the Viet Minh in North Vietnam or go into hiding in Cambodia. More than one thousand Cambodian Communists, including Son Ngoc Minh and Tou Samouth, chose North Vietnam. (Tou Samouth, however, soon returned to Cambodia.) Another thousand, including Saloth Sar, went underground in Cambodia. They temporarily abandoned armed revolution and began trying to influence Cambodia politically. Sar secretly entered Phnom Penh. He pretended to be an assistant to a Viet Minh officer who stopped in the city on his way to North Vietnam. Sar did not go to North Vietnam, though. He stayed in Phnom Penh when the officer left.

It seemed to some Cambodian Communists as if the Viet Minh had abandoned them. If the Cambodian revolution were to continue, it would have to happen without Vietnam's help. So after his return to Phnom Penh, Sar became actively involved in KPRP activities there. He joined the KPRP's Phnom Penh Party Committee, which was headed by another rising Cambodian Communist, Nuon Chea. Sar also helped set up the Pracheachon Party, an officially recognized political party that would run in the 1955 elections. Pracheachon served as a cover for the KPRP, letting the Communists keep their affiliations secret while fielding candidates for the election.

Sar's responsibilities included secretly coordinating Pracheachon and Democrat efforts. The Democrats had re-formed, and their leadership now contained people who had been members of the Marxist Circle in Paris. The Democrats were still popular, and they expected a Democrat or Democrat-Pracheachon government. Both the Democrats and the Pracheachon Party stressed the importance of setting up a democratic government (government by the people) according to the Geneva Conference. They also criticized Norodom Sihanouk's acceptance of U.S. aid.

The king still considered the Democrats a threat, so he used various strategies to cripple them. First, in March 1955, he gave up the throne, leaving his father to replace him. Norodom Sihanouk then formed his own political party, the Sangkum Reastr Niyum (People's Socialist Community). He counted on his popularity to help Sangkum win the election. He was indeed quite popular. Traditionalists continued to revere the king. They viewed his surrender of the throne as a sign of his deep concern for the people and his strong desire to work for them.

Second, Norodom Sihanouk took a neutral position on the Vietnam War and the larger global conflict between Communist and non-Communist nations. The United States had begun aiding South Vietnam directly by providing money and military advisers, and ten-

NORODOM SIHANOUK *(CENTER)* **POSES WITH** his father, Norodom Suramarit, and his mother, Sisowath Kossamak, in 1955.

sions in South Vietnam were mounting. Fear that the king's acceptance of U.S. aid would suck Cambodia into a continued Vietnam War had drawn many voters to Pracheachon and the Democrats. But now Sangkum proposed a stance aimed to keep Cambodia out of the war.

Third, Norodom Sihanouk shut down several Communist and leftist newspapers and put some of their editors in prison. As the election neared, police and soldiers arrested—and in a few cases killed—Pracheachon and Democrat Party members. Election day brought numerous irregularities, such as voter harassment and missing ballot boxes in areas where Democrats were expected to win.

Norodom Sihanouk's tactics worked. Sangkum won all the assembly seats, and Sihanouk became the prime minister. The new government signaled hard times to come for the Communists. But Saloth Sar was prepared to overcome any obstacles that stood in the way of his ideals and his growing power within the Communist Party.

CHAPTER 2

P FROM OLITICAL WORK

NORODOM SIHANOUK'S RULE as "democratically elected" leader of Cambodia began successfully, and this success weakened Cambodia's Communist movement. Warfare in the countryside had ended, so farmers could produce plentiful food. These farmers mostly owned the land they worked. Relatively few were landless, exploited tenants—people who farmed others' land for low wages and who received none of the farms' profits. Tenant farmers found Communism particularly attractive in other countries, but this class was small in Cambodia. In fact, most Cambodian peasants still staunchly supported the royal family. In the cities, unemployment was low and jobs were plentiful. Dissatisfied laborers—another class typically attracted to Communism—could simply quit their jobs and look elsewhere for work. Norodom Sihanouk took credit for these social improvements, as well as for independence and the

TO ARMED STRUGGLE

end of French taxes. He was so popular that Communists could no longer openly criticize him if they wished to gain supporters.

Norodom Sihanouk's policies made the Communists look unnecessary. By maintaining Cambodia's neutrality, he managed to get aid from both Communist and non-Communist countries. He spoke against Americans while accepting their aid, and he began a program of government efforts for the public good, such as opening new schools and hospitals. He labeled this program "Socialist," a term also used to describe many Communist government programs. (In a Socialist society, the means of production are owned not by individuals but by groups of workers or the nation as a whole. Socialism is one of the main goals of Communist revolutions.) As a result of these policies, Cambodian relations with Communist countries improved. These factors all brought him more support from the left.

REDS

During the French Revolution (1789–1799), a red flag became an important symbol of the French revolutionaries. Other revolutionaries in later years also took up red flags as their symbols. Eventually leftists, especially Communists, came to be labeled Reds.

Many Democrats joined the Sangkum Party. Even some Communist leaders began to feel that their struggle wasn't worthwhile.

One of these was Sieu Heng, a top Cambodian Communist. In 1955 Sieu Heng made a secret deal with Norodom Sihanouk. This deal exposed many important Communists, whom Norodom Sihanouk saw as threats to his power. At that time, the rural Communist movement was stronger than the urban one. Sieu Heng, who led the rural Communists, agreed to tell the government who the other rural leaders were. Until 1959, when Heng left the Communists, the government regularly raided Communist offices and killed or intimidated Communist staff. This crackdown on the Communists—or "Khmers Rouges" (Red Khmers), as Sihanouk called them—practically destroyed the rural party. Saloth Sar later claimed, "About 90 percent of our revolutionary forces in the countryside were destroyed in 1959, due to assassinations, arrests, recantations [withdrawals], and surrender to the enemy."

These difficulties contributed to Saloth Sar's rise in the party. The KPRP was quietly growing in Phnom Penh, but it had to work very secretly. Known leaders could not act openly. The head of the KPRP Central Committee, Tou Samouth, spent much of his time away from the city. Other well-known, high-ranking Communists (those who had run in past elections) were lying low for fear of arrest. As a result, Sar took on ever more important roles. A new leadership group arose, including Saloth Sar, Ieng Sary, and their fellow Marxist Circle member Son Sen.

Saloth Sar led a double life during this period. While he rose secretly in the KPRP under various pseudonyms, he also maintained a public face. As Saloth Sar, he got a job teaching several subjects at Chamroeun Vichea, a private high school. He was a popular teacher whose students found him eloquent, refined, friendly, and gentle. One student later recalled his lecturing style: "He spoke in bursts without notes, searching a little, but never caught short, his eyes half-closed, carried away by his own lyricism. . . . The students were subjugated [overpowered] by this affable professor, invariably dressed in a short-sleeved white shirt and dark blue trousers." Although Sar didn't include his political views in his lectures, he presented the ideal Communist persona: polite, well-educated, well-groomed, modest, and compassionate toward the poor. He wasn't alone in this endeavor. In fact, many secret Communists taught in Cambodian high schools in the 1950s. Son Sen and his wife, Yun Yat, got jobs at the Sisowath School, where Ieng Sary also taught. Ieng Thirith and Khieu Ponnary were teachers too.

"*The students were subjugated [overpowered] by this affable professor. . . .*"

—Soth Polin, one of Saloth Sar's students at Chamroeun Vichea, 1988

A BASTILLE DAY WEDDING

Saloth Sar and Khieu Ponnary married on Bastille Day (July 14), a holiday marking the beginning of the French Revolution in 1789. This anniversary was popular among Communists because French Revolutionary ideals—liberty, equality, and fraternity—were so similar to Communist goals.

In 1956 Saloth Sar married Khieu Ponnary. Meanwhile, Ieng Thirith taught extra classes to support the publication of Communist newspapers. The Communists' teaching and publishing efforts helped strengthen the KPRP in Phnom Penh. Schools churned out young idealists who had Communist role models and might join the KPRP, and popular newspapers spread their ideas. These newspapers included *Pracheachon*. Like the political party by the same name, this paper was a public face of the secret Communist Party. By 1958, 20 percent of the Khmer-language papers sold were Communist.

Many of the students who graduated from high schools where Communists taught became teachers in rural schools. These footholds among idealistic young Cambodian intellectuals were essential to the KPRP's survival. Norodom Sihanouk's political tactics had dried up other recruitment sources.

Norodom Sihanouk intimidated not only rural Communist leaders but also his opponents in Phnom Penh. Before a 1958 election, he decided to make sure the Democrats could not compete with his Sangkum Party. After a "debate" consisting mostly of bitter speeches about the Democrats, he ordered his guards to beat the

Democrats' leaders. During the next few days, similar beatings occurred all over Phnom Penh. The message was clear: to run against Sangkum was to endanger life and limb.

Norodom Sihanouk chose all sixty-two of the Sangkum candidates for the national assembly. He included some leftists to keep the support of left-leaning voters. Only five Pracheachon candidates ran, and four of them gave up before the election due to intimidation.

Naturally, the Sangkum candidates all won. The lone Pracheachon candidate, Keo Meas, got several hundred votes, but not enough to beat his Sangkum opponent. Given Norodom Sihanouk's attitude toward challengers, Keo Meas decided he'd be safer in hiding. He soon left for the countryside. His departure left a vacancy at the top of the KPRP's Phnom Penh branch. Saloth Sar filled it.

CAMBODIAN COMMUNIST PARTY REORGANIZATION

In 1960 the KPRP faced challenges that led to a major reorganization. Some of these challenges came from the government. Norodom Sihanouk ordered the police to shut down several leftist newspapers and arrest a number of suspected Communists in Phnom Penh. Those arrested included Saloth Sar's high school classmate and Marxist Circle comrade Khieu Samphan. This situation heightened the party disarray caused by Sieu Heng's 1959 defection to the government.

Other challenges came from within the Communist Party. Before 1960 older veteran independence fighters dominated KPRP leadership. Many of these men had close ties with Vietnam and had withdrawn there after the Geneva Conference. They favored working politically and opposed taking up arms against Norodom Sihanouk's regime because they appreciated his popularity and achievement of independence. They also recognized that his neutrality minimized U.S. influence in Cambodia.

In the early 1960s, younger party members, such as Saloth Sar, gradually came to dominate KPRP leadership. These members tended to be anti-Vietnamese and revolutionary. They favored armed struggle against Norodom Sihanouk, whom they saw as an old-fashioned, obsolete monarch who had to be overthrown for the good of modern Cambodia.

Changes in the Vietnamese Communist Party also contributed to reorganization among the Cambodian Communists. In 1960 Vietnamese Communists held a Party Congress and decided to resume armed struggle in South Vietnam. They planned to work with Cambodian Communists so North Vietnam could help South Vietnamese Communists by sending soldiers and weapons to South Vietnam via Cambodia. This meant armed revolution in Cambodia would once again take a backseat to the Vietnam War.

The KPRP followed the Vietnamese Party Congress with its own secret Party Congress in a Phnom Penh railway station. "It was in this bleak situation that we successfully convened our Party's First Congress, right in the railroad yards of Phnom Penh itself," said Saloth Sar in a speech seventeen years later. "In such a tense situation, with the enemy intensifying its repression, the participation of twenty-one representatives at the Party Congress was, in itself, a life-and-death struggle. Had the enemy discovered the site of the Congress, the entire leadership of the Party would have been destroyed, the line of the Party would never have seen the light of day, the revolution would have been gravely endangered and its future jeopardized."

These twenty-one representatives renamed the KPRP the Workers' Party of Kampuchea (WPK). They also elected new party leaders. Tou Samouth remained in the number one position. Nuon Chea took the second position, and Saloth Sar took the third position. Other elected leaders included Ieng Sary, Keo Meas, Son Ngoc Minh, and So Phim.

Though the WPK's leadership included some younger members after the 1960 Party Congress, older members still outnumbered them. The Party Congress made few changes to the party's policies. The WPK continued to stress national independence and oppose the United States. It approved armed struggle along with political efforts but kept working only politically for several years. However, Cambodians at least appeared to lead this reorganization, unlike the ICP and KPRP, whose establishment the Vietnamese Communists had initiated.

The 1962 election brought further reorganization of WPK leadership. As the election approached, Norodom Sihanouk turned his eye on Sangkum's only 1958 rival, Pracheachon. He arrested several Pracheachon Party members and the editor of the *Pracheachon* newspaper. Despite these actions, some Communists still wanted to contest the election via the Pracheachon Party. Others, including Saloth Sar, felt that running candidates in an election they couldn't win was a waste of valuable Communists. After losing an election, Sangkum opponents had to disappear for their own safety.

Shortly before the election, a key event ensured that the WPK sided with Saloth Sar. Tou Samouth was kidnapped and probably murdered. No one knows for sure who arranged this act, but its result was pivotal. Saloth Sar bypassed Nuon Chea to assume Tou Samouth's position at the top of the WPK leadership.

Cambodian Communists continued to teach and spread their message. Many young Cambodians turned against the Sangkum government, which had been elected in an uncontested race. In February 1963, students in the city of Siem Reap staged an antigovernment riot. This spurred the Communists to hold another Party Congress. This one confirmed Saloth Sar as the WPK's party secretary (top leader). It also removed from the Central Committee some prominent Communists who believed in continuing political struggle rather than armed struggle. Ieng Sary's rank rose, and another former Marxist Circle member, Son Sen, joined the Central Committee.

Saloth Sar, Ieng Sary, and Son Sen left their teaching jobs to devote themselves full-time to WPK administration. The younger party members had overpowered the older ones, and they began focusing the party's efforts on agitating against Norodom Sihanouk's regime and preparing for military action. The party still found most of its support among Cambodia's intellectuals, thanks to Norodom Sihanouk's "Socialist" policies. These policies had increased education but hadn't modernized the economy. As a result, Cambodia had an ever-growing number of educated young adults who couldn't get jobs. This economic climate produced the sort of dissatisfaction that led many youths to Communism.

Though the WPK was invigorated, its leadership in Phnom Penh was in danger. Soon after the Siem Reap riots, Norodom Sihanouk assembled a list of people he suspected of scheming against the government. The list included Saloth Sar and Ieng Sary. In May 1963, they went into hiding and devoted themselves to preparing for an armed Communist revolution. They left their wives behind in Phnom Penh and headed east for Kampong Cham Province. They planned to set up their Communist base there. For the next several years, they spent most of their time in eastern Cambodia and in Communist-controlled territory in South Vietnam, organizing and preparing for a war against Norodom Sihanouk.

THE VIETNAM WAR ESCALATES

Meanwhile, events in Vietnam were making Norodom Sihanouk's neutrality harder and harder to maintain. Choosing either Vietnamese side (Communist or non-Communist) would infuriate its Cambodian opponents and raise tensions between Cambodia's left and right. Inevitably, one side would gain the upper hand, and Norodom Sihanouk would no longer be able to play the sides against each other.

In November 1963, assassins killed South Vietnamese president Ngo Dinh Diem. Norodom Sihanouk believed that the United States (which publicly supported the unpopular Diem) was behind the assassination, and this belief made continued U.S. aid personally dangerous for Sihanouk. Also, the United States could use its aid to Cambodia as leverage to draw Cambodia into the Vietnam War on the non-Communist side. Furthermore, Sihanouk became convinced that South Vietnam would fall to the Communists. So his policies at the end of 1963 took a sharp left turn. First, he ended all U.S. aid. To replace it, he drew closer to Communist countries such as China and North Vietnam. He also let Vietnamese Communists move through Cambodia. In return, Vietnamese Communists promised to recognize Cambodia's borders if they won the Vietnam War.

The Vietnam War continued to escalate. The United States had been supporting South Vietnam with military equipment and advisers since the 1950s. The advisers could fight back if attacked—and sometimes did more than that—but the United States wasn't technically a full participant in the Vietnam War. That changed in 1964, when U.S. officials claimed that North

POSTERS ATTACKING FOREIGN INTERVENTION HANG ABOVE A PHNOM PENH
branch of the Ministry of Information in the early 1960s. The posters support the
king's decision to terminate relations with the United States.

Vietnamese boats had attacked two U.S. naval ships in the Gulf
of Tonkin. The United States began bombing North Vietnam and
then increased bombing raids in 1965. It also bombed Communist
bases on Vietnam's border with Cambodia, making the area
unsafe for Cambodian Communists. Hundreds of thousands of U.S.
troops came to South Vietnam.

As the United States became more involved in the Vietnam War
and Norodom Sihanouk tried to stay out of it, Saloth Sar traveled to
North Vietnam and China. He found little support for a Cambodian
revolution in either place. Vietnamese Communists insisted that

Cambodians should help them win the Vietnam War before starting their own revolution. China was supporting Norodom Sihanouk, so it couldn't devote resources to a revolution against him.

But Saloth Sar's 1965 trip to China did have some impact. First, China noticed the rivalry between Cambodian and Vietnamese Communists. At the same time, relations between China and the Soviet Union, the world's largest Communist powers, were very strained. North Vietnam had recently grown closer to the Soviet Union. Saloth Sar's appeal to China offered China a way to counterbalance Soviet influence in Indochina.

Another important aspect of Saloth Sar's trip to China was the chance to see its society firsthand. Sar visited at the beginning of China's Cultural Revolution, when Chinese Communist leader Mao Tse-tung launched a campaign to purge (arrest or otherwise remove) his party enemies and to reorganize society according to what he considered pure Communist principles. This revolution greatly impressed Saloth Sar.

While Norodom Sihanouk's policies continued shifting to the left, Cambodia's national assembly began shifting to the right. Conservative members lamented the loss of U.S. aid. They also predicted that Norodom Sihanouk's recent nationalization (government takeover) of banks and international trade would ruin Cambodia's economy.

In the 1966 elections, Norodom Sihanouk kept a low profile. He didn't select Sangkum candidates for the assembly this time. Few of his 1962 picks ran again and kept their seats. Three secret Communists working with Sangkum (Khieu Samphan, Hou Youn, and Hu Nim) were reelected. Overall, though, the election led to a conservative national assembly. The assembly chose Lon Nol, a popular army general detested by Communists, as prime minister.

CHINA'S CULTURAL REVOLUTION

Saloth Sar insisted that Cambodia's Communist revolution was uniquely Khmer and had no foreign models. However, he greatly respected China's Communist leader Mao Tse-tung, and China's Cultural Revolution from 1966 to 1976 seems to have made a strong impression on Sar.

In 1965 and 1966, Mao thought rival factions within China's Communist Party were growing too powerful. He also believed that a return of capitalism loomed. To counter these trends, he and his associates began a movement called the Cultural Revolution. Its purpose was to wipe out China's old ways and promote Mao's revolutionary thought.

The movement quickly spun out of control and turned bloody. It purged both innocents and Mao's opponents from China's Communist Party, destroying party leadership. It also led to a social upheaval enforced by terror. It sent intellectuals to do manual labor in the countryside, while young soldiers destroyed private property and terrorized people who weren't "properly revolutionary," such as people wearing Western clothes or people thought to favor some capitalism in Chinese society.

After Mao Tse-tung's death in 1976, China's Communist Party concluded that the Cultural Revolution was Mao's biggest mistake. This mistake was Saloth Sar's key model for revolutionary Communist government.

THE SAMLAUT UPRISING

Norodom Sihanouk's economic reforms did cause problems. For one thing, a large rice export black market arose in response to trade nationalization. Farmers illegally sold much of Cambodia's rice to Vietnamese Communists, who paid more than the Cambodian government. As a result, the government lost a lot of export income. To regain it, Lon Nol set up a system whereby the army collected rice crops. This system forced farmers to accept very low prices.

The new rice collection system started in Battambang Province. Unlike most of Cambodia, where farmers worked their own land, Battambang had many large landowners and lots of tenant farmers. Because people felt oppressed by their landlords, Communism had become more popular there than in some of the other provinces.

Many Battambang residents rose up against Lon Nol's soldiers. Saloth Sar's Communists probably had no direct control of the uprising. In fact, they considered it premature. "The people armed themselves with knives, axes, clubs and other weapons they could lay their hands on to attack police stations and military garrisons," Saloth Sar later

LON NOL SERVED IN CAMBODIA'S police and military before becoming prime minister in 1966.

explained. "[But t]he Party Central Committee had not yet decided on general armed insurrection [uprising] throughout the country." The most notable uprising occurred at Samlaut, an area about 15 miles (24 kilometers) from the city of Battambang. On April 2, 1967, rebels killed two soldiers there and took their rifles. Rebel numbers grew that day as they marched carrying banners denouncing the government. They proceeded to attack guard posts and capture more weapons.

Throughout Cambodia government, retaliation was rapid and ruthless. People evacuated villages in areas where they feared government soldiers would approach. Soldiers arrested hundreds of rebels and people accused of belonging to the Khmer Rouge. (Government officials and outsiders had begun using this name for the Cambodian Communists and all who fought on their side.) The government executed a number of detainees. Norodom Sihanouk accused the three Communists in the national assembly of supporting the rebellions. All three disappeared into the countryside that year.

The Samlaut uprising had made Cambodia a dangerous place for Communists. But it also created the conditions Saloth Sar had been waiting for: widespread opposition to the government that could explode into a national revolution. Sar moved the headquarters of Cambodia's Communist Party—which had changed its name to the Communist Party of Kampuchea, or CPK—from eastern to northeastern Cambodia. He established a new base in the mountainous jungle of Ratanakiri Province to prepare for war. He found staunch supporters in the Khmer Leou, the hill tribes who lived there.

Foreign Communist regimes kept treating Norodom Sihanouk as an ally. Even as he pursued Cambodian Communists, he continued to let Vietnamese Communists escape through Cambodia from U.S. and South Vietnamese maneuvers. He also allowed the North Vietnamese to receive shipments of Chinese weapons at the Cambodian port of Sihanoukville. The North Vietnamese could transfer the weapons to Communist soldiers in South Vietnam from Sihanoukville. In return, Lon Nol received a portion of those weapons for the Cambodian military.

Since they lacked support from Communists in other countries, Cambodian Communists began their revolution independently. They set up bases in the countryside where antigovernment feelings were strong and where they could attack government forces. The Khmer Rouge divided Cambodia into several zones, each commanded by the Communist leadership at that zone's base. In theory, the Central Committee in the northeastern zone commanded all the zones. In practice, however, the zones were fairly independent. Saloth Sar explained part of the reason the zones had to act independently: "All contact involved at least a month's delay, since it meant a trip on foot or by elephant, and it was constantly necessary to evade the enemy to avoid ambush."

The Khmer Rouge began its offensives in 1968. Most of these actions were small-scale efforts to capture government guns. To succeed without external aid, they needed to capture a lot of guns. Saloth Sar later claimed that at the end of March 1968, the Khmer Rouge had only ten guns for the entire northeastern zone.

Though the Khmer Rouge was relatively weak, Norodom Sihanouk began to feel seriously threatened. This threat sent him swinging back to the political right, toward conservative Cambodians and the United States. He sent Lon Nol's army against the Cambodian Communists. The army didn't find the Central Committee, but it killed 180 Khmer Leou and 30 Khmer

Rouge. Norodom Sihanouk also began suggesting that Vietnamese Communists were supporting the Khmer Rouge.

Actually, Cambodian and Vietnamese Communist cooperation varied from zone to zone. In the eastern zone, Cambodian Communists worked closely with the Vietnamese Communists who sheltered there. Eastern zone Communists put Cambodian operations on hold as the Vietnamese prepared for their upcoming Tet (New Year) Offensive, a major military campaign against South Vietnamese and U.S. forces. Saloth Sar, however, resented North Vietnam's continued insistence that Vietnam's revolution should precede Cambodia's. As he organized actions in the northeastern zone, he refined his ideal of a self-reliant, independent Cambodian revolution. As a result, the northeastern zone began its antigovernment offensive earlier than the eastern zone. Other zones did too.

When the Khmer Rouge attacked, Norodom Sihanouk had Lon Nol respond with air strikes and counterattacks. When government soldiers caught up with rebels, they cut off the rebels' heads and displayed them in public areas as a warning.

In 1968 Vietnamese Communists launched the Tet Offensive. The Tet Offensive went poorly for Vietnamese Communists, and many fled into Cambodia. Their Cambodian bases and the Ho Chi Minh Trail (a system of routes through Laos and Cambodia by which North Vietnam supplied South Vietnamese Communists) became even more important to them. U.S. president Richard Nixon responded by ordering a massive secret bombing of these areas. The bombing began in March 1969. Thus the Vietnam War began to spill across Cambodia's border, further destabilizing the country.

Norodom Sihanouk's response to the bombing seemed inconsistent. While protesting the bombing, he reestablished diplomatic

BLAST CIRCLES MARK BOMB STRIKES after U.S. planes attacked a Cambodian town near the Ho Chi Minh Trail in 1969.

relations with the United States. At the same time, he officially recognized the Provisional Revolutionary Government established by South Vietnam's Communists. In return, Vietnamese Communists promised to remove their troops from Cambodia when the Vietnam War was over. Though these acts appeared at odds with one another, they allowed Norodom Sihanouk to avoid taking sides—and avoid fighting either North Vietnam or the United States directly.

SIHANOUK LOSES CONTROL

Despite Norodom Sihanouk's efforts to keep control of Cambodia, his power was rapidly slipping away. The Communist revolution was gaining strength in Cambodia's countryside, and the Vietnam War had spread there too. Even in Phnom Penh, the situation looked grim. Cambodia's economy was faltering, and Norodom Sihanouk was losing political support from both the right and the left.

Cambodia's population was growing, but farm production hadn't increased since the 1940s. Cambodia hadn't effectively developed its industrial sector either. So when landless people moved to the cities, they couldn't find jobs. Furthermore, global prices for rubber, Cambodia's main export, were falling. At the same time, rubber production was dropping due to U.S. bombings and rural unrest. One effort to stimulate the economy, a casino in Phnom Penh, brought mixed results. It earned the government some income but also caused a rash of bankruptcies and suicides among gamblers.

All these problems troubled conservatives. Meanwhile, rural military crackdowns and silencing of urban dissenters vexed liberals and intellectuals. Some traditionalists still respected Norodom Sihanouk as royalty. But even that respect was fading. He had abolished some valued traditions while assuming a "democratic" appearance, and Cambodians were also growing accustomed to hearing calls for an end to his rule.

Norodom Sihanouk had always worked tirelessly at governing, but he began to give up that effort. He spent more time enjoying himself and indulging in hobbies, such as moviemaking. In August 1969, Lon Nol and Prince Sisowath Sirik Matak, both friends of Cambodian conservatives and the United States, formed a new national assembly. Then, in January 1970, Norodom Sihanouk left Cambodia to rest and seek medical care in France.

GROWING REVOLUTION

Between 1967 and 1970, the Khmer Rouge made great strides in territorial control and recruitment. By 1970 it fielded more than five thousand soldiers—about one-seventh the number of Cambodian government soldiers. It had also gradually occupied about 20 percent of Cambodia's countryside. But its attacks remained sporadic and mostly rural. It wasn't yet prepared to seize national power.

In late 1969, Saloth Sar returned to North Vietnam, once again seeking support for his revolution. Vietnam's Communist leaders and Cambodian Son Ngoc Minh (who served on the CPK's Central Committee from Vietnam) tried to slow him down. They urged him to suspend Communist military activities in Cambodia while the Vietnam War continued. They also tried to persuade him to form connections with the Soviet Union's Communist Party, as Vietnam had. But Sar was determined to continue his armed struggle in Cambodia. And hoping for support from China, he refused to ally with the Soviet Union.

Saloth Sar had devoted half his life to Communism. All that time, he had worked to bring about a revolution that would create an independent Communist Cambodia. While Cambodia had gained independence, hereditary royalty still governed the country. Many government officials were rich capitalists (people who favor a market economy and private ownership of property) and corrupt bureaucrats (government officials) who worked not to improve the lives of the people but to enrich themselves. To Saloth Sar, it seemed that these political parasites filled the cities and sucked up Cambodia's wealth, leaving nothing to the peasants who produced it. By 1970 he believed that Cambodia needed a Communist revolution more than ever before.

"BRIGHT RED BLOOD

THE OPPORTUNITY FOR A FULL-BLOWN COMMUNIST REVOLUTION in Cambodia developed from 1970 to 1975 via Cambodia's shifting political and military landscape. First, a coup by Lon Nol in Phnom Penh produced an alliance between Norodom Sihanouk and the Cambodian Communists. This alliance in turn formed a coalition government (a temporary alliance of different governments to achieve a common goal) in exile (outside Cambodia) and a military front (a coalition of armed forces) to regain Phnom Penh. Repression by Lon Nol's government and events related to the Vietnam War drove many rural Cambodians to join the fight against Lon Nol. And Communism grew more appealing to rural Cambodians. They saw U.S. bombs destroy lives and livelihoods, while Communists fought against U.S. causes and for a society that would provide food and other necessities for everyone.

"WHICH COVERS TOWNS AND PLAINS"

ALLIANCE WITH THE KING

While Norodom Sihanouk was in France, Cambodian conservatives took advantage of his absence to act independently. Lon Nol and Sisowath Sirik Matak's government closed the casino and privatized the banks (changed them into companies under private control). They stepped up military activity against Cambodian Communists. They also began kicking Vietnamese Communists out of Cambodia. The government staged massive protests against Vietnamese Communists in the border provinces and Phnom Penh. It also cut off supplies to Vietnamese Communists in Cambodia and South Vietnam. Then, on March 13, 1970, Lon Nol demanded that all Vietnamese Communist troops leave Cambodia within two days.

A CAMBODIAN PROTESTER IN MARCH 1970 SMASHES AN OVERTURNED
vehicle belonging to North Vietnam's embassy in Phnom Penh. The Cambodian
government encouraged such anti-Vietnam demonstrations.

Despite Lon Nol and Sisowath Sirik Matak's defiance, Norodom
Sihanouk remained in charge—in name, at least. But he guaran-
teed his own ouster while planning a return to Cambodia. While he
agreed to make efforts to remove Vietnamese Communist soldiers
from Cambodia, he considered Lon Nol's demands rash. Norodom
Sihanouk would first travel to Moscow and Beijing. In these two
capital cities, he would urge the Soviet and Chinese governments to
pressure North Vietnam into withdrawing from Cambodia. On March
14, before he left France, he privately said he planned to have cer-
tain government members executed upon his return. Sisowath Sirik
Matak found out about this plan and revealed it to Lon Nol and the
national assembly. Lon Nol and Norodom Sihanouk's other opponents
agreed to overthrow him. On March 18, 1970, surrounded by tanks
and soldiers, the national assembly approved a new government.

The assembly's president, Cheng Heng, would be temporary head of state. Lon Nol would remain prime minister, and Sisowath Sirik Matak would assist him. The assembly also declared a state of emergency (pronounced that the situation required extraordinary governmental powers to deal with it) and gave Lon Nol the power to take action.

North Vietnam and China refused to recognize the new Lon Nol government, which sided with the United States and intended to keep preventing the supply of South Vietnamese Communists via Cambodia. North Vietnam and China continued to recognize Norodom Sihanouk as Cambodia's head of state. When Sihanouk arrived in Beijing, Chinese officials helped him form an exile government that would oppose Lon Nol.

Saloth Sar had also traveled to Beijing seeking support for Cambodia's Communist revolution after Vietnam's rebuff. Sar was still in Beijing when Norodom Sihanouk arrived there. Sar participated in China's negotiations with the deposed king but didn't meet with him personally. When the meetings ended, Norodom Sihanouk announced by radio that he was forming an exile government, the National Union of Kampuchea. He called Cambodians to rebel against Lon Nol's government. He also announced an alliance with Cambodian Communists, hoping their ongoing fight would return him to power. Khmer Rouge fighters would join pro-Sihanouk groups in Cambodia and form a National Unified Front (the Front, for short) to liberate Cambodia from Lon Nol. North Vietnam still believed winning the Vietnam War should precede Cambodia's Communist revolution. But North Vietnam supported Norodom Sihanouk, so its troops in Cambodia would also support the Front.

To outside observers, the structure of the National Union of Kampuchea and the Front were unclear. Norodom Sihanouk was head of state, and his relationships with Chinese and North

Vietnamese officials were very important. However, Sihanouk spent most of the civil war years living out of sight in Beijing. In Cambodia, Khieu Samphan was the highest-ranking official of the coalition government. He had served in Norodom Sihanouk's government before Lon Nol's coup, so he appeared to be Sihanouk's representative in Cambodia. But Khieu Samphan was still a Communist, and the highest-ranking Cambodian Communist was Saloth Sar. Only central members of the CPK knew who actually headed it. Lower-level party members and nonmembers knew nothing about Saloth Sar's status. His official position in the coalition with Norodom Sihanouk was military commander of the National Unified Front. This position enabled him to fill the military with Communists.

VIETNAM WAR SPILLOVER

As the National Unified Front began its activities, Vietnam War spillover into Cambodia escalated. Soon after Lon Nol's coup, South Vietnamese forces and Kampuchea Krom Khmer fighters advised by Green Berets (U.S. Army Special Forces) began to enter eastern and southern Cambodia. At the same time, Vietnamese Communist forces occupied northeastern Cambodia. In fact, the South Vietnamese Communist command center had moved to Cambodia to avoid destruction.

From April to June 1970, the United States and South Vietnam launched a full-scale invasion into eastern Cambodia searching for this Communist command center. Although Lon Nol had requested U.S. help against the Vietnamese Communists, the United States did not warn him about the invasion. First, U.S. and South Vietnamese planes dropped hundreds of tons of bombs on Cambodia. Then tens of thousands of U.S. and South Vietnamese troops followed. They failed to find the Communist command center, which simply moved west as the invasion advanced.

The United States soon withdrew its ground forces. But about eight thousand South Vietnamese soldiers remained in Cambodia. Nixon explained the U.S. withdrawal by saying the United States had no treaty obligation to defend Cambodia. To justify the continued South Vietnamese presence, he said, "What they are doing is cleaning out some of the sanctuary areas [safe havens for Communists] that were not completed when we left."

Cambodians saw their countryside being destroyed by a Vietnamese war in which neither side respected Cambodian territory. Vietnamese Communist troops occupied more and more Cambodian land and villages as they moved westward. The South Vietnamese forces operating against the Communists in Cambodia gained a reputation for banditry. So Lon Nol's call to force the Vietnamese Communists out of Cambodia met widespread Cambodian support.

Volunteers flooded the Cambodian army. It grew from 35,000 to about 150,000 soldiers during 1970. But the army trained these volunteers hastily, and they were ill-prepared to fight the Vietnamese Communists. Thousands of Cambodian troops died in the effort to push the Vietnamese out of Cambodia. These losses, combined with the U.S. and South Vietnamese invasions, ignited anti-Vietnamese hatred among Khmer people in Phnom Penh. In April and May, the city's police and soldiers slaughtered hundreds of Vietnamese civilians—men, women, and children. This massacre in turn brought South Vietnamese retaliation.

CAMBODIAN SOLDIERS FIRE ON A VILLAGE SAID TO HIDE VIETNAMESE
forces. Thousands of civilians died in anti-Vietnam actions in Cambodia.

While Lon Nol's army expanded, support for the Khmer Rouge also increased. Several factors helped Communism grow popular in Cambodia. Most importantly, U.S. and South Vietnamese bombing of Cambodian civilians spurred thousands of Cambodians to fight for the Communists against Lon Nol's pro-American government. Also, while Phnom Penh had accepted Lon Nol's coup fairly easily, the countryside still backed Norodom Sihanouk. When Communists rebroadcast Sihanouk's Beijing radio address in rural Cambodia, support for the Khmer Rouge surged. Since the "king" and the Communists were working together, traditionalist peasants could support them both. Furthermore, three popular (and secretly Communist) former assembly members—Khieu Samphan, Hou Youn, and Hu Nim—called the people to support the Communist-Sihanouk coalition. In response to this call, masses of people demonstrated in several rural areas and towns. The army quashed these riots, arresting thousands of people and killing hundreds. This repression backfired on Lon Nol, driving more Cambodians to join the Communist revolution.

By late 1970, Cambodia was teeming with troops. The National Unified Front fielded about 115,000 soldiers: 15,000 fought with the Khmer Rouge, 60,000 fought in non-Communist units, and 40,000 were Vietnamese Communists. Lon Nol's army was bigger than the Front by 35,000 soldiers, but they were poorly trained and dying by the thousands. About 40,000 non-Communist South Vietnamese soldiers further complicated the military situation in Cambodia.

Cambodia's Communist revolution benefited from the Vietnamese Communists in Cambodia. These well-trained veteran Vietnamese troops usually won confrontations with Lon Nol's rookies. Vietnamese Communist soldiers were also well disciplined, and they presented themselves as liberators in league with Norodom Sihanouk. They helped the Cambodian people see Communism in a positive light.

Nevertheless, several CPK Central Committee members, including Ieng Sary, Son Sen, and Saloth Sar, remained adamant that the Vietnamese and Cambodian revolutions must stay separate. These members overrode other Central Committee members, such as Nuon Chea, Hou Youn, and Son Ngoc Minh, who favored a joint command with Vietnam. Communication among Communist leaders in Cambodia's different zones remained difficult and intermittent, though, so cooperation with Vietnamese Communists continued to vary. In the eastern zone, Cambodian Communist leader So Phim didn't resist Vietnamese help. There the Vietnamese created schools for political, technical, and military training, and Cambodian and Vietnamese Communists worked together closely. Thanks to this close relationship, the eastern zone produced the best Khmer

Rouge soldiers. By contrast, the northeastern zone leadership, which included Ieng Sary and Son Sen, refused Vietnamese Communist offers of a military hospital, medical personnel, and other support.

Saloth Sar and his supporters distrusted not only the Vietnamese but also Khmer Communists who worked too closely with the Vietnamese. In June 1970, the one thousand Cambodian Communists who had taken refuge in North Vietnam after the Geneva Conference began to return. Upon their return, they had to sign a paper stating that they wanted to leave Vietnam's Communist Party and join the CPK. Even then the CPK put few of them in leadership positions, and they had to give up the military ranks they had earned in Vietnam. Most of them became common soldiers, despite the skills they had mastered through intensive training in Vietnam.

CAMBODIA'S CIVIL WAR

Though war raged in the countryside, many Phnom Penh residents were optimistic about Lon Nol's government during 1970. In September Lon Nol seemed to have some military success. He declared victory in Operation Chenla I, a major military offensive against the Vietnamese Communists. Lon Nol's troops had actually failed to dislodge the Vietnamese soldiers and had called in U.S. bombers to do the job. But even this situation looked promising to Cambodian conservatives, who saw it as a sign of U.S. support for Lon Nol. They believed U.S. aid and money would soon flow into Cambodia. They were right. U.S. military aid would increase ninefold at the beginning of the next year.

To boost Lon Nol's popularity, in October 1970, his government declared that Cambodia was a republic, which would have democratically elected rulers, rather than a monarchy. The government renamed the country the Khmer Republic. Those who had opposed the royal family welcomed this change. Lon Nol also released Norodom Sihanouk's political prisoners. The newspapers Sihanouk had shut down could print again. Lon Nol was popular at first, but he wasn't the type of skilled leader who could steer Cambodia out of the difficulties it faced. His faith lay in Buddhist mysticism and Khmer racial superiority, which he thought would overcome all the country's problems.

And the war was far from over. The Communist-led National Unified Front and its Vietnamese Communist allies were making great strides in the countryside. Nixon thought the U.S. Air Force wasn't doing enough against Vietnamese Communists there. In December 1970, he told his national security adviser, Henry Kissinger, to order a massive air strike: "I want them to hit everything. I want them to use the big planes, the small planes, everything they can that will help out here and let's start giving them a little shock."

The Front and the Vietnamese Communists launched military campaigns each year, conquering more and more territory. In January 1971, Vietnamese Communist forces destroyed most of Cambodia's air force in an attack on the Pochentong Airport near Phnom Penh. The ruined aircraft included all the Cambodian military's fighter jets and four helicopters. The stress of the war took its toll on Lon Nol. He had a stroke soon after the airport attack. He recovered but had to spend two months convalescing in Hawaii. After the stroke, his mystical beliefs played an even stronger role in his decisions. Then, in October 1971, the Front wrested Cambodia's valuable rubber plantations from South Vietnamese troops. The same month, the Front attacked and defeated Lon Nol's Operation Chenla II force protecting the highway between Kampong Thom and Phnom Penh. Lon Nol staged no more major offensives after that defeat.

The Communists kept up their recruitment strategies. These included youth-oriented propaganda meetings. Young people came away from these meetings excited about a redistribution of wealth. Communist recruitment was particularly successful in areas such as the southwest, where there were lots of poor peasants who liked the idea of collective labor. And, of course, the Communists' anti-American stance attracted more and more Cambodians as U.S. bombing continued. Although the Front had

A TROOP OF FEMALE KHMER ROUGE SOLDIERS MARCHES TO BATTLE.

Bit Boeun *(fifth from left)* left her farm to join the rebels in 1971. Under the Khmer Rouge, she was a tailor, a farmer, and a janitor, as well as a soldier.

begun as a coalition of groups opposed to Lon Nol, Communists dominated it over time.

From 1971 to 1973, the CPK worked hard to establish itself as the chief social and administrative power in Cambodia's "liberated" areas (where Lon Nol had no control). It instructed cadre (people who had undergone Communist Party training) to be courteous and helpful to villagers. The CPK impressed people with its discipline and ideals of equality. At the same time, it downplayed Norodom Sihanouk's role in the resistance, claiming that the successes were due to Communist efforts. But it didn't openly oppose non-Communist groups in the coalition. When North Vietnam and China wanted Sihanouk to tour the liberated areas, the CPK obliged. Cadre treated him respectfully as they guided him through their territories from February to April 1973.

Meanwhile, the CPK leadership grew increasingly anti-Vietnamese. Some military cooperation with Vietnamese Communists continued, especially in the eastern zone and in actions against South Vietnamese forces. But after multiple snubs from North Vietnam, Saloth Sar insisted more strongly than ever that Cambodia's revolution should be self-sufficient. In 1971 the CPK Central Committee closed the eastern zone Vietnamese schools. And though few of the Cambodian Communists who had returned from North Vietnam were in leadership positions, the CPK removed them from power.

The people of Phnom Penh, who had largely welcomed Lon Nol's coup at first, grew disenchanted as they saw his regime's corruption and ineffectiveness. The city was crowded with refugees. As the Front seized more and more of the countryside, it began to blockade the cities and often managed to cut off supplies. Politicians grew rich on U.S. aid, but commoners suffered and other income dwindled. The Khmer Republic had lost control of the rubber plantations. No rice was available for export. Farming had nearly ground to a halt.

The republic held elections in 1972 (in areas it controlled) so Lon Nol could become president. He had become terribly unpopular. His brother had to rig the elections to ensure Lon Nol's victory. The only real choice was between the unpopular U.S.-backed Lon Nol and a Communist takeover. To those who opposed Communism, there seemed no acceptable choice at all.

In late 1972, participants in the Vietnam War reached a cease-fire agreement. As a result, both Communist and non-Communist Vietnamese forces withdrew most of their soldiers from Cambodia. However, U.S. bombings there quintupled. In 1973 the United States dropped more than 257,000 tons (more than 233,000 metric tons) of bombs on Cambodia. The bombing continued even though U.S. intelligence had discovered that it increased Communist ranks. By the time the U.S. Congress finally halted funding for the bombing in August 1973, the United States had dropped more than 500,000 tons (more than 453,000 metric tons) of bombs on Cambodia, killing up to 150,000 civilians in addition to the targeted Communist soldiers. In one case, a B-52 jet bombed Neak Luong, a town held by the republic, killing government soldiers and nearly 100 civilians. Because of all these civilian casualties, Communist recruiters had no trouble convincing Cambodian villagers that Lon Nol had requested the air strikes and must be deposed.

After the bombing stopped, Cambodia's civil war remained deadlocked. Lon Nol's forces still couldn't go on the offensive. The Front, for its part, remained unable to take Phnom Penh. It had suffered greatly during the final U.S. bombing campaign, and the Vietnamese and their equipment had withdrawn. The

Front controlled more than 75 percent of Cambodia. But at that time more than 50 percent of the population resided in the cities, because more than 750,000 refugees had fled to Phnom Penh and the provincial capitals. The republic still governed the majority of the population, but it held only Phnom Penh, some provincial capitals, and part of the northwest.

Although the Front couldn't take Phnom Penh, it could blockade the capital. Also, with the U.S. bombings stopped, the Front could shell Phnom Penh. It did so in 1973 and 1974. Once the shelling began, food could reach the capital only via the Mekong River or by air.

SURVIVORS OF A KHMER ROUGE SHELLING ATTACK ON PHNOM PENH
walk through a devastated neighborhood in early 1974.

LIFE IN LIBERATED AREAS

In the countryside, Communists began announcing that Cambodia had become a Socialist regime. They urged people to work and fight for Socialism. The Central Committee instructed cadre to "make the people understand that they are to have a gun in one hand and a plough in the other."

One aspect of Socialism for which the Communists believed some areas were ready was agricultural collectivization. Under this system, no one would own the land and everyone would work together to produce food for the common good. This effort met mixed reactions. Before the war, most peasants had owned their land. Land was a valuable private asset for many reasons. And if farmers produced more food than they needed, they could sell it. Under collective agriculture, landowners would give up their property and surplus food would go to the government. Thus, collectivization was quite a sacrifice for some Cambodians. On the other hand, hundreds of thousands of people were displaced and

"Make the people understand that they are to have a gun in one hand and a plough in the other."
–Cambodia's Pre Veng Province Committee to provincial cadre, 1974

starving. Something had to be done to revive farming and feed the nation. Collectivization began to help this effort.

Not all Khmer Rouge practices in liberated areas were meant just to establish Socialism. Once the Vietnamese withdrew, the Khmer Rouge no longer had to feign friendship with them. It began referring to them as enemies. It began killing ethnically Vietnamese Cambodian civilians, just as Lon Nol's regime had. The Khmer Rouge also began executing Cambodian Communists who had returned from North Vietnam.

The Khmer Rouge attacked not only Vietnamese people but also other non-Khmer ethnic groups. It eliminated ethnic Thai members from the CPK, in many cases killing them. It also began to persecute Cham people.

KHMER ROUGE FIGHTERS KILLED THIS FAMILY DURING A RAID ON A VILLAGE of ethnic Vietnamese Cambodians in 1974.

The Khmer Rouge counted among its enemies not only Lon Nol's soldiers and non-Khmer ethnic groups but also Khmer people it considered "class enemies." As smaller cities surrendered to the Khmer Rouge, it began to demonstrate who class enemies were. It killed many Khmer capitalists and intellectuals because the Khmer Rouge considered these people real or potential counterrevolutionaries—people who would move to return to a capitalist society. It sent those who weren't enemies of some sort, or who were enemies that the Khmer Rouge thought it could redeem (such as some intellectuals and shopkeepers), to work in the fields.

Poor rural people were generally eager to join the Communists. Whereas the poor had been powerless before the revolution, the Khmer Rouge promised to place them in the most powerful local positions. The CPK also strengthened its public support by taking young teenagers to indoctrination (teaching) camps. The youths emerged opposed to religion, parental authority, Cambodian traditions, and capitalism. Like many other Communist groups, the CPK believed that religion and other customs, as well as traditional family relationships, sustained old ways of thinking and had to be eliminated. Some youths joined the Khmer Rouge simply because, as soldiers, they "didn't have to work, and could kill people." These indoctrinated teenagers dedicated themselves to Angkar, the secret rulers of the revolution.

Angkar referred to the CPK's leadership, and increasingly only to party secretary Saloth Sar and deputy secretary Nuon Chea. The CPK, which claimed about four thousand members in 1970, grew to about fourteen thousand during the following five years. By this time, the Front—dominated by Communists—was poised to take Lon Nol's final strongholds: Phnom Penh and Battambang.

FINAL BLOWS

Throughout 1974 Phnom Penh held out against the Front. Then Norodom Sihanouk made a deal with China to buy water mines (bombs that would explode when ships touched them) with Cambodia's rubber profits. Front soldiers placed these on the Mekong River in early 1975 and kept shelling the capital.

With mines in the Mekong, only U.S. planes could bring food, ammunition, and other supplies to Phnom Penh. But airlifts couldn't provide enough food for the millions of people there. These people anxiously awaited the city's inevitable liberation. They had no idea what to expect, other than the end of Lon Nol's regime. Crowded, starving, and exhausted, many secretly longed for the advance on Phnom Penh that would end the war. And the Front continued to close in.

International politics affected how the Cambodian civil war—like many other events in Cambodian history—ended. In February 1975, U.S. president Gerald Ford predicted that "the Cambodian army will run out of ammunition in less than a month" and "[g]overnment forces will be forced, within weeks, to surrender to the insurgents" unless the U.S. Congress approved emergency funding to supply Lon Nol. At that point, Ford hoped not that the Cambodian government could beat the Communists but simply that it could hold out a little longer and reach a "negotiated settlement."

But Lon Nol refused to negotiate a settlement with Norodom Sihanouk. U.S. diplomats and Cambodian politicians pressured Lon Nol to leave the country so someone else could negotiate. Finally, after the Cambodian government offered him one million dollars and declared him a national hero, Lon Nol left Cambodia with his family on April 1, 1975. He traveled first to Indonesia and then

GLORIOUS APRIL 17

The first verses of Cambodia's national anthem under Saloth Sar celebrate the day Khmer Rouge soldiers finally conquered Phnom Penh:

Bright red Blood which covers towns and plains
Of Kampuchea, our Motherland,
Sublime Blood of workers and peasants,
Sublime Blood of revolutionary men and women fighters!

The Blood changing into unrelenting hatred
And resolute struggle,
On April 17, under the Flag of the Revolution,
Frees from slavery!

Long live, long live Glorious April 17!
Glorious Victory with greater signification
Than the times of Angkor!

to Hawaii for medical treatment. The day Lon Nol left, the Khmer Rouge took Neak Luong, one of the last government military bases defending Phnom Penh. The United States evacuated by air most of the Americans remaining in Phnom Penh on April 10.

After taking Neak Luong, Khmer Rouge soldiers converged on Phnom Penh. On April 16, a radio broadcast by the National

Unified Front cried out, "Beloved brothers, sisters, workers, youths, students, teachers, and functionaries. Now is the time! Here are our Cambodian People's National Liberation Armed Forces, brothers! . . . Rebel! . . . It is time for you to rise up and liberate Phnom Penh." Backed by heavy rocket and artillery attacks, the Khmer Rouge closed in on the capital that night.

At nine o'clock in the morning of April 17, 1975, the government military command in Phnom Penh decided to surrender. It could not announce the surrender by radio, because the radio station workers had fled. Officials instead announced the surrender by flying white flags from government buildings. The Khmer Rouge immediately occupied Phnom Penh. On the same day, they occupied Battambang too.

Saloth Sar exulted in this victory. Though no one but the CPK's inner circle knew it, Sar headed Cambodia. At last, he could reorganize Cambodian society according to his ideals. "For more than two thousand years, our people lived in disgrace and in the darkest shadows, without any light," he later explained. "Then the daylight shone. The brightest day of all for our people was April 17, 1975."

CHAPTER 4

DEMOCRATIC

WHEN THE KHMER ROUGE CONQUERED PHNOM PENH, Saloth Sar and his CPK inner circle began reorganizing Cambodian society according to their ideals. The CPK shared many ideals, such as classless collectivism, with other Communists and liberal thinkers around the world. Communist revolutions in other nations had clearly affected Cambodian Communists. And Vietnamese Communists had provided essential support to help Cambodian Communism develop.

However, the CPK insisted that its revolution was original and uniquely Cambodian. "We have no model for building up our new society," Saloth Sar later proclaimed. His "unique" Khmer approach and stubborn self-reliance contributed to Cambodia's problems. So did his determination to change Cambodia immediately and thoroughly and to protect his own power. Putting the poorest and

KAMPUCHEA

A CHILD SOLDIER OF THE KHMER Rouge patrols the streets of Phnom Penh after the city surrendered on April 17, 1975.

least educated people, as well as inexperienced teenagers, in roles of power led to widespread human rights abuses. A rigid chain of command, in which superiors held absolute authority over subordinates, led to chronically inaccurate reporting and constant blaming. This blaming made it seem as if enemies were everywhere. And to the Khmer Rouge, all enemies—real or imagined—had to be eliminated.

URBAN LIBERATION

Author and activist Loung Ung was a child during Cambodia's civil war and Saloth Sar's regime. In a book about her experiences, she describes the arrival of Khmer Rouge soldiers in Phnom Penh: "Everyone suddenly stops what they are doing to watch the trucks roar into our city. Minutes later, the mud-covered old trucks heave and bounce as they pass slowly in front of our house. Green, gray, black, these cargo trucks sway back and forth on bald tires, spitting out dirt and engine smoke as they roll on. In the back of the trucks, men wearing faded black long pants and long-sleeve black shirts, with red sashes cinched tightly around their waists and red scarves tied around their foreheads, stand body to body. They raise their fists to the sky and cheer. Most look young and all are thin and dark-skinned, like the peasant workers at our uncle's farm, with greasy long hair flowing past their shoulders."

SOCIETAL REORGANIZATION

On April 17, 1975, Khmer Rouge soldiers spread throughout Phnom Penh. Most of them wore black uniforms, but eastern zone soldiers wore gray or khaki. Different troops from Cambodia's various Front-controlled zones occupied different sections of the city and treated residents differently. The eastern zone soldiers were generally the best disciplined and among the last to demand that the people evacuate. Yet despite these differences, all troops received orders from the same mysterious Angkar.

As the Khmer Rouge began its tasks in Phnom Penh, residents noticed something chilling. Besides some cheering as they entered the city, the soldiers showed little joy or triumph. They just grimly set to work searching for military officers and high-ranking officials in Lon Nol's government. These people were marked for execution.

To the Communists, winning Cambodia's civil war was only the first step in the revolution. The next step was evacuating the cities. The CPK believed urban dwellers were parasites, living off the rural harvest and giving nothing back. Within a week of Phnom Penh's surrender, the Khmer Rouge forced nearly three million people to leave Phnom Penh, Battambang, and several other cities. It sent these people to the countryside to farm rice, just as it had done with residents of towns conquered earlier. Some soldiers told evacuees that the United States, which had supported Lon Nol, would begin bombing Cambodia's cities. Other soldiers gave no explanation. In some areas, soldiers gave people time to load their belongings on carts or into cars. In others, soldiers told people to pack enough food to wait out a few days of bombing. In still other areas, soldiers told people to take nothing and leave immediately.

The CPK announced additional reasons for urban evacuations. Saloth Sar's official explanation said that the cities lacked food and that city residents were needed in the countryside to increase rice production. This explanation seemed reasonable to many city dwellers, as years of war had crippled Cambodia's agriculture. Saloth Sar also explained that the cities contained U.S. and Vietnamese spies. Emptying the cities would isolate these spies and render them powerless.

Public rationale aside, the CPK had three main reasons for

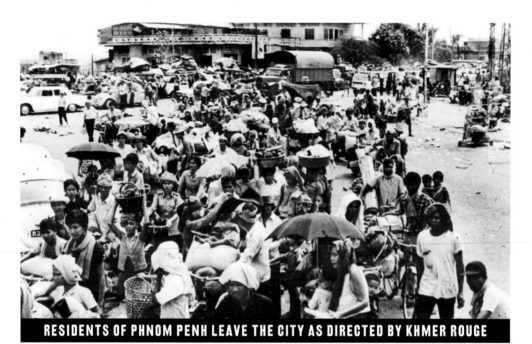

RESIDENTS OF PHNOM PENH LEAVE THE CITY AS DIRECTED BY KHMER ROUGE forces in 1975. They leave on foot or bicycle with only a few possessions.

evacuating Cambodia's cities. The first two were ideological. The CPK believed that urban parasites should either become productive agricultural workers or die. Evacuations also helped the Communists abolish private property by removing people from their land and homes. The third reason for evacuation was practical. The CPK had experience controlling the countryside, but it had no experience in urban administration. The CPK would have to rely on nonrevolutionaries to govern the cities if they remained intact. But such experts didn't belong to the working class. They weren't manual laborers or peasant farmers. They were members of an elite class intolerable to the CPK's version of Communist society.

The CPK called urban evacuees "new people" or "April 17 people." It called people who already lived in the countryside "old people" or "base people." As April 17 people filed out of the cities, cadre required them to write "biographies." The Khmer Rouge used these biographies to identify class enemies (people who weren't laborers or peasants) and political enemies (people who had worked for Lon Nol's government or military). It took away these enemies for "education"—which often meant secret execution.

At first many people wrote truthful biographies. Educated urbanites who did so may have believed that the Khmer Rouge was trying to identify useful skills for rebuilding the nation. Or these people may have believed that Khmer Rouge education meant, at worst, political indoctrination. But clever evacuees quickly realized they had better claim to be peasants or factory workers.

The Communists also made other major changes to Cambodian society. Soon after their military victory, they began to abolish money and prohibit buying and selling. They believed that with no private property, workers wouldn't need money. And with no money, the corrupt elite could no longer exploit the people. The people would work on cooperative farms, and the farms would distribute food to their workers. The government would also give each worker a new set of clothes annually.

The CPK's wartime command zones became the basis for the new government's administrative zones. A CPK leader commanded each zone. Zone commanders had to obey Angkar's orders unconditionally. But where they had no specific orders, they could govern independently. Zone commanders chose local leaders from among the very poor, the landless, and the uneducated. Local leaders had to obey zone commanders and Angkar without question, but where they had no specific orders, they held absolute power. This authority included the power to condemn people to death.

Though no aspect of Cambodian society—from the length of people's hair to the color of their clothes—went untouched by the

CPK, it kept its membership and structure secret. The CPK had little trouble maintaining secrecy. Most Cambodians—especially April 17 people—were afraid to be too curious. And cadre used pseudonyms, so it was difficult to connect the names of public officials with the names of party members. Even within the party, leaders told members only what they needed to know.

MILITARY MISHAPS

In the weeks after April 17, military communication between Phnom Penh and distant areas of Cambodia remained difficult. Vietnam War bombings had destroyed many communications facilities and roads. Messengers became more necessary than ever—and took longer than ever. Slow communication led to events that nearly caused war between Cambodia and two stronger enemies: Vietnam and the United States.

The Cambodian civil war ended two weeks earlier than the Vietnam War, so a non-Communist South Vietnam still existed in late April 1975. Some CPK naval commanders operating in the Gulf of Thailand decided to take advantage of this situation to gain territory for Cambodia (possibly under orders from the CPK inner circle). After Phnom Penh surrendered, naval units moved in on some South Vietnamese islands. Fighting over the islands continued even after North Vietnam's final victory on April 30.

Meanwhile, another event in the Gulf of Thailand further destabilized Indochina. The new Cambodian government's navy seized the U.S. cargo ship *Mayaguez*, which was carrying military equipment to Thailand. The United States demanded return of the

Mayaguez within twenty-four hours. But no countries had diplomatic contact with the new Communist regime in Phnom Penh, and communication between the navy and CPK leaders was slow.

When CPK leaders heard about the *Mayaguez* seizure and the U.S. demand, they announced via radio that Cambodia would return the ship. The announcement did not say what would happen to the crew. U.S. president Ford ordered a mission to recover the ship and crew. Two hundred U.S. marines landed on the island of Koh Tang, where they thought the Khmer Rouge was holding the *Mayaguez* crew. U.S. bombers also destroyed Cambodian naval and air force equipment and the country's oil refinery. But Cambodia had already abandoned the *Mayaguez* and freed its crew, who were headed to the mainland on a Thai fishing boat. Altogether, thirty-eight marines died in the fighting—mostly after Cambodia returned the *Mayaguez* and its crew.

Saloth Sar was unprepared for a foreign war. He wanted to focus on Cambodia's internal revolution. So in June 1975, he went to Hanoi, the capital of reunified Vietnam, to discuss the Cambodia-Vietnam border. Although the visit left many issues unresolved, it helped prevent eruption of a major

U.S. MARINES STORM ABOARD THE *Mayaguez* to recapture it from the Cambodian navy.

conflict with Vietnam. The new Cambodian government also officially apologized to the United States for the *Mayaguez* incident.
This apology allowed the United States to consider the incident
over. In Cambodia the incident reminded the Khmer Rouge that
the United States remained an enemy.

MORE SOCIETAL CHANGE

As Cambodia's external crises settled, Saloth Sar and his inner
circle turned their attention inward. Determined to rebuild the war-
torn nation and establish the ideal of Khmer self-sufficiency, they
continued to carry out a total reorganization of Cambodian society.

To improve agricultural production, they believed they had to
redistribute the country's population. They wanted to maximize
production in the fertile northwest. To that end, cadre in the southwest loaded people—many of them displaced April 17 people—
onto trucks and freight trains. These they sent north to establish
labor camps. "They put us on a very crowded train, where we had
to squat on the floor with our knees up, packed together for many
hours. When it was time to get off the train, I couldn't straighten
my legs or stand up," recalled one forced immigrant. In total, these
moves increased the northwestern population by about eight hundred thousand people.

The Communists also organized mobile brigades of single
young men and women. These brigades worked on large projects,
such as building dams and irrigation systems. The work brigades
contained both April 17 people and base people.

On collective farms and in work brigades, everyone worked

long hours. Many April 17 people were unused to manual labor. Sometimes base people helped April 17 people adjust to farm life. But base people often looked down on April 17 people. And new local leaders often forced April 17 people to work longer hours than base people. Exhaustion and malnutrition led to many injuries and illnesses, especially among April 17 people.

At first people generally accepted the necessity of hard work. Bombs had destroyed Cambodia's fields and roads. Everyone could see that Cambodia needed massive efforts to rebuild. But even though nearly the whole population was working to increase food production, the amount of food available to Cambodians—particularly to April 17 people—did not grow. In 1975 China provided the Cambodian Communist regime with rice and medicine as well as military equipment. But by 1976, the new Cambodian government was demanding so much Chinese military aid that Cambodia had to pay for it somehow. Though Cambodia still wasn't producing enough food for its own people, the government began shipping rice to China in return for China's military aid. Cambodian Communists refused to acknowledge China's help. They claimed that Cambodia's revolution was original and uniquely Khmer and that Cambodia was entirely self-sufficient.

This insistence on self-sufficiency and uniquely Khmer approaches—unevenly applied and sometimes illogical—added to hardships in the countryside. For example, the CPK rejected nonmilitary aid, such as shipments of DDT, a pesticide used to control mosquitoes. As a result, the mosquito-borne disease malaria spread widely. Communist Cambodia's medical system was another example of counterproductive Khmer-centric policy. Few doctors trained in Western medicine (medical care as generally practiced in Europe and North America) remained in Cambodia.

Most had fled, hidden their class identities, or died by execution. And the Khmer Rouge distrusted imported ideas such as Western medicine, so medical workers were largely untrained peasants who relied on folk remedies. Saloth Sar later boasted that after the first few years of Communist rule, "each cooperative has its own medical center and its own center of making traditional, national and popular medicines." This claim may have been true. However, the medical personnel were unskilled, and the medicines were generally ineffective. Furthermore, the Khmer Rouge often denied April 17 people even this basic medical treatment.

PURGING ENEMIES

As Cambodia's society transformed, the Khmer Rouge continued to purge enemies of the revolution. These foes included all class enemies and most non-Khmer people.

While moving people to collective farms and work brigades, soldiers and cadre rooted out class enemies. Class enemies were capitalists (people who ran businesses or lent money), imperialists (all foreigners and people of non-Khmer ethnic groups), feudalists (royalty and Buddhist priests), and bourgeoisie (middle-class citizens and intellectuals). The Khmer Rouge either forced class enemies into especially hard labor or killed them.

Class enemies who reached farms or work brigades without being discovered still were not safe. Having a relative who had been a capitalist or a bureaucrat, for example, could lead to denunciation at any time. One brigade member recalls, "Every day several of our companions were 'called.' They never came back, which

KHMER ROUGE SOLDIERS STAND GUARD OVER SUSPECTED "CLASS ENEMIES" as they do hard labor on a canal near Battambang in 1976.

means that the Khmer Rouge had massacred them. . . . For them, we were all traitors because we had been officials. Aside from peasants and workers, all others deserved death."

Execution or hard labor did not befall every single class enemy. In some places early in the Communist regime, people suspected of opposing CPK ideals might go to reeducation camps. There cadre exposed them to party propaganda. These people did have to work, but in some cases, the party let them spend the nights with their families and provided sufficient food. This kind of reeducation dwindled over time.

Xenophobia (fear and hatred of everything foreign) among the Khmer Rouge led to additional oppression of non-Khmer people. Even unfounded claims of Khmer Communists spying for foreign powers could lead to imprisonment, torture, and execution.

Saloth Sar and his associates believed Vietnam and the United States were Cambodia's main enemies. His regime kept persecuting and deporting Vietnamese Cambodians, just as Lon Nol's regime had. The Khmer Rouge expelled more than one hundred thousand Vietnamese people. It also blamed any opposition to Cambodia's Communist regime on Vietnamese and U.S. spies. Soldiers took people accused of working for Vietnam or the United States to an interrogation center called S-21 in Tuol Sleng, a suburb of Phnom Penh. In 1975 the Khmer Rouge tortured and killed about two hundred prisoners in its effort to force confessions of Vietnamese and U.S. espionage (spying).

Other ethnic groups suffered too. For example, many Muslim Cham people were offended by the Khmer Rouge's abolition of religion after April 17. A number of Cham people protested or even rebelled against the Khmer Rouge. The Khmer Rouge responded by slaughtering Cham villagers wherever this occurred. To discourage further rebellion, the Khmer Rouge sent residents of other Cham villages to live in Khmer cooperatives and placed Khmer immigrants in Cham villages, scattering more than 150,000 Cham people throughout the northern and northwestern zones. There they faced even greater risk of execution than Khmer residents. Speaking a

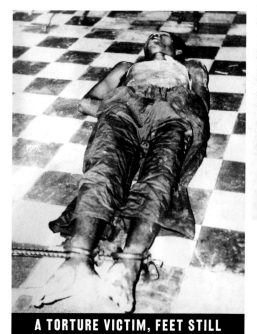

A TORTURE VICTIM, FEET STILL shackled, lies on the floor at the S-21 interrogation center.

TUOL SLENG

After the Khmer Rouge evacuated Phnom Penh, it converted some buildings there to new purposes. In the suburb of Tuol Sleng, the Khmer Rouge converted a set of school buildings into a center for torture and execution. This center went by the code name S-21.

Secret police brought accused traitors or enemies of the CPK to S-21, where guards kept them chained in tiny cells. The Khmer Rouge tortured the prisoners to force them to admit crimes, such as spying for Vietnam or the United States, and give up the names of their accomplices. The confessions were often false, given in hopes of ending the torture. Nonetheless, interrogators kept detailed records of these confessions and used them to locate more "enemies."

As more confessions led to more enemies and as Pol Pot grew ever more paranoid, S-21 processed more and more people. In 1975 five hundred people came to Tuol Sleng. In 1976 that number rose to more than sixteen hundred. By 1979 more than sixteen thousand people had entered S-21's torture cells. Since guards tortured the accused until they confessed and since the punishment for political enemies was execution, a trip to Tuol Sleng nearly always ended in death. Ultimately, only about a half-dozen prisoners emerged alive.

In 1979 the People's Republic of Kampuchea (successor to Democratic Kampuchea) converted S-21 to yet another purpose. It became a museum, to help people remember the atrocities that happened there.

language other than Khmer, such as the Cham language, was illegal. So was eating differently from others, such as refusing pork when it was available. (Islam, the religion of the Cham people, forbids eating pork.) Execution was the punishment for these crimes.

POLITICS AND PARANOIA

The cities stayed empty, except a small quarter of Phnom Penh. Here the government kept factories and workshops running. It even called back some evacuated workers, including a few educated professionals, to operate specialized equipment. It also established a new government headquarters in Phnom Penh.

During the months after April 17, the Communists in Phnom Penh renamed their country Democratic Kampuchea. They also created a new national constitution. This constitution overturned traditional Cambodian society. It banned private property, including the family farms at the heart of most Cambodian communities. Agricultural collectives would replace family farms. The new constitution also outlawed religion, including Buddhism, the core of Cambodian beliefs and values. The constitution defined all citizens as peasants, workers, or soldiers and described their duties as building and defending the country. Yet it did not mention Socialism or Communism.

"Our aspiration is to edify [build] a society where happiness, prosperity and equality prevail for everybody, a society where there are neither exploiting class nor exploited class, neither exploiting people nor exploited people."

—Pol Pot, describing the goals of Democratic Kampuchea to reporters, 1978

Throughout 1975 the new government's leadership remained shrouded in mystery. Norodom Sihanouk, the figurehead of Cambodia's exile government, returned home in September 1975. But he was by no means in charge. In fact, he spent most of his time abroad performing diplomatic tasks for Democratic Kampuchea.

Saloth Sar, the real power behind Angkar, stayed out of sight. He kept using pseudonyms, as he had ever since leaving his teaching job to be a full-time revolutionary. He wore the same black uniform worn by the workers, peasants, and soldiers. He feared assassination and always employed a large staff of bodyguards. He kept several houses and slept in a different one each night so assassins wouldn't know where to find him. Chronic stomach problems convinced him that someone was trying to poison him.

The CPK kept its existence and its control of Democratic Kampuchea secret, even when it established an official government in 1976. It put on a show to make the new government appear democratic. In January 1976, the CPK had Norodom Sihanouk declare that the new constitution, which abolished royalty, was taking effect. He then resigned to spend the rest of the Democratic Kampuchea years under house arrest. The constitution called for ratification (approval) by a national assembly, so an election took place in March. But all the candidates were secret CPK members.

The national assembly "chose" a prime minister almost no one had heard of: a man named Pol Pot. Pol Pot was Saloth Sar's latest pseudonym. At first only his intimate Communist friends recognized Pol Pot as the Saloth Sar who had taught school in 1950s Phnom Penh. Nuon Chea became head of the national assembly. Khieu Samphan became president of the state presidium (an executive committee common to many Communist governments).

With Communists firmly in control of the government and an

POL POT *(LEFT)* **STANDS WITH FELLOW KHMER ROUGE LEADERS**
(from his left) **Nuon Chea, Ieng Sary, and Son Sen in Phnom Penh in about 1976.**

army of more than sixty-eight thousand preventing counterrevolution, Pol Pot continued to consolidate his power in the CPK. His grudge against Vietnam and inaccurate information from his subordinates led him to believe that enemies filled the party. So from 1976 to 1978, he conducted a series of purges. Khmer Rouge soldiers and security police arrested CPK members in zones Pol Pot considered too influenced by Vietnam. They also arrested purged members' relatives. These arrests generally led to execution.

Among Pol Pot's perceived party enemies were those who considered 1951 the founding year of Cambodia's Communist Party. Vietnamese Communists had established the Khmer People's Revolutionary Party in 1951. To Pol Pot, people who commemorated the KPRP this way were pro-Vietnamese traitors. Pol Pot considered 1960 the founding year of Cambodia's Communist Party. That was the year twenty-one Cambodian Communists had held a Party Congress in a Phnom Penh railway station and formed the Workers' Party of Kampuchea. It was also the year Pol Pot and Ieng Sary had joined the Central Committee.

Within the CPK, Pol Pot was developing a group loyal to him above all else. He considered loyalty to himself and his ideology more important than friendship and shared experiences. Two of the first major figures to fall in his purges were Ney Saran, the north-eastern zone party secretary, and Keo Meas, a former CPK Central Committee member. Both of these men had been Pol Pot's close associates since the 1950s. But in September 1976, he had them arrested and sent to the S-21 facility in Tuol Sleng.

Four months later, Khmer Rouge agents arrested two more important party members and forced them to confess to working with the U.S. Central Intelligence Agency (CIA). Since both of these men had strong connections in the northern zone, Pol Pot concluded that "treacherous, secret elements buried inside the Party" had been infiltrating the CPK for years. He decided to search the northern zone for these elements. A purge of CPK officials and military officers there lasted throughout 1977.

The purge soon spread to the northwestern zone. In this zone, Ieng Thirith, Democratic Kampuchea's minister of social affairs, had recently observed great misery. She explained, "In Battambang, I saw that they made all the people go to the rice fields. The fields were very far away from the villages. The people had no homes and they were all very ill. . . . I know the directives of the Prime Minister were that no old people, pregnant women, women nursing babies, or small children were to work in the fields. But I saw everybody in the open rice fields, in the open air and very hot sun, and many were ill with diarrhea and malaria." Such conditions were common in Democratic Kampuchea. But local officials feared reporting bad news to their superiors, because execution was Pol Pot's punishment for failing at one's job. So top leaders often didn't realize the effects of their policies. When Ieng Thirith saw the situation with her own eyes, she couldn't believe it. Rather than acknowledging the real cause of such misery—forced mass immigration and unrealistic demands for agricultural production—she blamed it on foreign agents among the northwestern zone's party members. A purge followed. Replacement cadre and officers came from the southwestern zone, which Pol Pot considered loyal to him. Chhit Choeun, a skilled military leader who avoided taking sides in CPK politics, commanded the southwestern zone. He used the pseudonym Ta (Grandfather) Mok. Ta Mok's authority thus grew as the purges continued.

Another problem plagued Pol Pot's information about happenings in the countryside. One of his primary sources was "confession" extracted under torture from alleged agents of Vietnam and the CIA. Hoping to stop their torture, the accused all admitted to working for Vietnam or the United States. Few, if any, were actually spies. But Pol Pot's subordinates told him that the prisoners had confessed, so he believed the CPK was full of spies.

FOOD SHORTAGES

Executions weren't the only deadly aspect of Pol Pot's regime. His agricultural policies also killed a lot of people. During the first years of his rule, Pol Pot focused on farming—primarily rice production. In 1976 Democratic Kampuchea stepped up agricultural

POL POT ON RICE PRODUCTION

In a March 17, 1978, interview with Yugoslavian journalists, Pol Pot painted an unrealistically rosy picture of life in Democratic Kampuchea: "The first outstanding result is that we have solved the agricultural problem, especially in rice-growing. To have the problem of rice production solved means to have enough rice to feed our people. In 1976 . . . [the rice yield] allowed us to solve the living conditions of our people and also to export rice. . . . [I]n 1977, we had a paddy production higher than that in 1976. We could then improve the living conditions of our people and export more rice."

collectivization and created a four-year production plan. This plan was extremely unrealistic. It called for doubling or tripling rice production, even on lands that had never yielded that much rice. And the CPK's insistence on uniformity and equality often reduced yields. For example, all rice paddies had to be the same size, no matter what the local conditions were. Also, farms throughout the country had to plant the same strain of rice, even when locally bred strains better suited to an area were available.

Nevertheless, Pol Pot believed cooperative farming could work miracles. He thought that once people were working for the common good, rather than the profit of capitalists, productivity would skyrocket. "Where can we find the capital to build our industry?" he asked. He then answered, "Our capital comes essentially from the work of our people. Our people, by their work, develop agricultural production. . . . We also have another important source of capital. That is the fact that we have no salary. The absence of salary constitutes in itself a great source of capital." Pol Pot believed that the only people who actually received significant salaries before the revolution were useless "functionaries." The common people received little or nothing in exchange for their labor. Therefore, not paying salaries saved money that had been wasted before the revolution.

Even as Democratic Kampuchea failed to feed its people, it continued to export rice. As a result of food shortages, tens of thousands of people—especially April 17 people—died of starvation as well as overwork and disease made worse by malnutrition. According to one villager, food was so scarce that "people ate lizards and geckoes," and disease was so common that "even some of the gravediggers died on the job."

Pol Pot's agricultural policies and political purges aggravated each other. Angkar's production plan led local leaders to demand more and more from overworked people. Meanwhile, to protect themselves, local leaders had to exaggerate how much food they were producing. National leaders then believed their policy was succeeding. When they discovered the truth, they purged local leaders. The replacement leaders then demanded even more from the exhausted workers.

BORDER TENSIONS

As Pol Pot enacted his domestic policies, relations between Democratic Kampuchea and its neighbors grew strained. Violence began to erupt on its borders. Thailand strengthened its military border guard. In response, the Khmer Rouge attacked the Thai forces. It attacked Laotian border guards as well.

After the Cambodian civil war and the Vietnam War ended, border skirmishes with Vietnam continued through 1976 and 1977. In early 1977, these conflicts increased, although neither country admitted that it was at war. Angkar ordered local leaders to arrest Vietnamese-speaking Khmer people and the few Vietnamese Cambodians remaining in Democratic Kampuchea. Many of the latter were women married to Khmers. Local leaders interpreted arrest orders as execution orders, and another anti-Vietnamese massacre ensued.

Amidst these conflicts, in September 1977, Pol Pot gave a five-hour radio speech. In this speech, he announced—more than two years after the Khmer Rouge had taken Phnom Penh—that the CPK governed the country and that he was its leader. For the first time, the CPK officially and publicly acknowledged its own existence. "In commemorating the Seventeenth Anniversary of its founding, our Party has decided to solemnly proclaim, before our country and the whole world, the official existence of the Communist Party of Kampuchea," Pol Pot declared.

Throughout 1976 and 1977, China continued to supply weapons and equipment to Democratic Kampuchea. With this Chinese support, four Cambodian divisions attacked Vietnam from late September through November 1977. The Cambodian commanders claimed that Vietnam had invaded and that they were simply repelling the aggression.

In response, Vietnam did invade in December 1977, with more than twice as many soldiers. The Vietnamese soon triumphed and withdrew, taking with them hostages who eventually joined other Cambodian exiles in Vietnam.

To Vietnam, the withdrawal was an attempt to negotiate a peace settlement with Democratic Kampuchea. Vietnam clearly had the upper hand. But to Pol Pot, the facts were unimportant. Vietnam's withdrawal provided an opportunity for Democratic Kampuchea to declare victory over its much stronger neighbor. Pol Pot did just that in a radio broadcast on January 6, 1978.

A FALSE UTOPIA

Though he had claimed victory over Vietnam, Pol Pot knew the truth. If Vietnam decided to invade in earnest, it could easily conquer Democratic Kampuchea. Pol Pot needed foreign allies to prevent this.

In 1977 and 1978, he allowed official diplomats from several countries, including some non-Communist Southeast Asian nations, to work in Cambodia. He also admitted Communist visitors from non-Communist countries such as the United States. Visitors could tour Angkor Wat and observe agricultural projects that showed Democratic Kampuchea's great progress. Cadre—often high-ranking CPK members—always accompanied visitors and showed them clean, happy, well-fed workers. These workers were actually cadre staging scenes.

IN 1978 POL POT AGREED TO meet with U.S. journalists for the first time. They took this portrait during the interview.

Another technique Pol Pot used to gain international support was pretending to reduce repression. The CPK declared a general amnesty (pardon) of April 17 people, as well as amnesty for several different types of domestic enemies, such as people who had worked for Sihanouk or Lon Nol before 1975. In 1978 the CPK celebrated its anniversary by hosting feasts throughout the country.

Democratic Kampuchea also tried to improve education. It established primary schools in many areas (although often only the children of base people could attend). The government made plans for a new technical college in Phnom Penh too. Some of its instructors would be intellectuals who had returned from abroad at the end of the civil war. These returnees had survived the initial purge of intellectuals and were doing hard labor in factories and on farms. Ieng Sary welcomed some of these survivors back to Phnom Penh.

Pol Pot assumed a more accessible persona. During his rare public appearances, he typically charmed his audiences, speaking "like a father to his children." But the public knew nothing about his background. In March 1978, he at last presented his autobiography via an interview with Yugoslavian journalists.

Cambodians knew these moves were nothing but show. Repression raged on as Pol Pot ordered a crackdown in the eastern zone, where he suspected a strong Vietnamese spy influence. Unlike earlier purges, this one met resistance. The zone commander, So Phim, defied Pol Pot's order. So in May, Ta Mok and Son Sen attacked with southwestern zone troops, killing thousands and sending even more to other zones for torture and execution. Most of these victims were peasants, the very people Pol Pot's revolution was supposed to help. So Phim committed suicide in June 1978 to avoid a similar fate.

Many survivors of the eastern zone purges fled across the border, where Vietnam had stationed about one hundred thousand troops since April. Cambodian refugees in Vietnam began to include Khmer Rouge soldiers and leaders as well as peasants. Many refugees joined Hun Sen, a former Khmer Rouge leader who had defected to Vietnam in 1977. The Vietnamese welcomed Cambodian refugees, trained them for future military actions against Democratic Kampuchea, and helped them form an exile government. Vietnam also began providing more support to dissenters in the eastern zone.

Purges continued in other zones. So did murders of CPK leaders Pol Pot considered failures and extermination of class enemies.

The Khmer Rouge collected new biographies from April 17 people. Then it executed those with antirevolutionary connections, such as people who had been teachers, soldiers in Lon Nol's military, or low-level government officials under Lon Nol. It continued to slaughter Vietnamese Cambodians, Khmer people from Kampuchea Krom, and other Vietnamese-speaking Khmer people. According to the CPK, "The Khmer Krom had all become Vietnamese—Khmer bodies with Vietnamese minds." The Khmer Rouge also labeled Chinese Cambodians, the nation's traditional shopkeepers and moneylenders, as capitalists and class enemies. It spared some Chinese Cambodians because it needed China's support. Even so, they suffered. In 1978 dozens perished in Tuol Sleng, while thousands more fled to China.

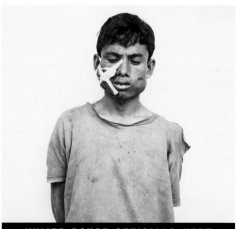

KHMER ROUGE OFFICIALS KEPT photographs as well as biographies of accused people. This man was tortured and killed in Tuol Sleng.

The Pol Pot regime had much in common with earlier revolutionary regimes in other countries and even with earlier Cambodian regimes. New regimes often eliminate their predecessors and political opponents. In Cambodia, for example, Norodom Sihanouk and Lon Nol had both imprisoned and killed political opponents.

Pol Pot's regime took this practice to the extreme. His revolution differed from others in its thoroughness. The Khmer Rouge imprisoned and executed not just direct or suspected opponents. It also killed those whose backgrounds suggested that they might not promote the revolution. Local Khmer Rouge leaders even murdered people who simply complained of exhaustion or hunger. Executions were generally shootings.

Pol Pot's regime also radically restructured Cambodian society. It eliminated urban life, redefined fundamental social units such as families, and forced nearly all its citizens to work from early morning until late at night. But instead of increasing productivity and equally distributing wealth, the regime's policies bred the worst hardship and violence Cambodia had ever experienced.

Democratic Kampuchea took a horrible toll on human life. No one knows for sure how many people perished in Pol Pot's Cambodia. Even the lowest estimates say that hundreds of thousands of people died of execution, disease, overwork, and starvation between April 1975 and January 1979. Most estimates place the death toll at more than one million, or about one-seventh of the nation's population. The dead included more than 25 percent of the April 17 people and more than 15 percent of the base people. Nearly 50 percent of Cambodian Cham people died. The regime killed or deported virtually all Vietnamese Cambodians.

Young Saloth Sar had envisioned a Communist utopia. As Pol Pot, he tried to make this dream a reality. His experiment failed.

CHAPTER 5

LIFE UNDER

AS THE KHMER ROUGE ASSERTED CONTROL over areas it conquered during the Cambodian civil war, Communists put in place a system of collective living. The main unit of society would no longer be the family. It would be the cooperative.

CITIZENS

Each cooperative would provide its people with the food, clothing, and shelter they needed. All the people in a cooperative would work together for the common good. And work they did, from morning to night. Workers spent their rare days off in propaganda meetings or self-criticism sessions. At self-criticism sessions, cadre encouraged

POL POT

WORKERS TEND RICE PADDIES AT A COMMUNAL FARM OUTSIDE
Phnom Penh in the mid-1970s.

and sometimes threatened people to talk publicly about things they had done wrong. These gatherings replaced visits to Buddhist temples. The Khmer Rouge abolished religion, and Buddhist monks and priests had to work in the fields like everyone else.

RARE
SUCCESSES

Michael Vickery, a scholar who interviewed many Cambodian refugees in 1980, cites a variety of experiences these refugees had in different areas. In some places, Pol Pot's regime seemed to have realized some of its ideals. That is, everyone had to work hard and live meagerly, but the people worked together. Even April 17 people lived no worse than peasants had before the revolution.

In one case, a law student evacuated from Phnom Penh and returned to his hometown, where he had to work in the fields. Even though he was an intellectual, his parents had some Chinese ancestry, and his father was a carpenter (not a peasant), his family survived the Pol Pot regime. The cooperative's full members did mistreat the family. But on the flip side, the former student—who had a reputation as a hard worker—received a three-month rest when he fell ill. He was also allowed to do an easy job as he recovered.

To house people equally in the cooperatives, the CPK ordered construction of new one-room dwellings. Each of these houses sheltered several families. Khmer Rouge soldiers destroyed large houses in the cities and in the country. These big homes represented corrupt luxuries enjoyed by enemies who exploited the people.

In the cooperatives in 1975, families generally managed to stay together. They worked long hours apart but ate their evening meals and spent their nights together. One of the CPK's policies, enforcing communal dining, eventually changed this situation throughout most of Cambodia. Communal dining tried to erase inequality and minimize individuality and privacy. Under this system, all a cooperative's people ate meals together, sitting with their workmates.

In many areas, the Khmer Rouge instituted communalism to an even greater degree, separating the sexes and severing family ties. The Khmer word for *family* took on a new meaning: "husband and wife pair." Though a married couple constituted a family in Democratic Kampuchea, husbands and wives worked—and in many cases lived—apart, in separate men's and women's groups. Where the CPK required couples to live separately, husbands and wives could visit each other only a few times per month.

The CPK strictly controlled the institution of marriage. Every union required party approval. Men could not marry before the age of thirty years except under special conditions. The party conducted mass weddings for dozens of couples at once. It also enforced strict regulations about interaction between single males and females and forbade sexual activity between unmarried people. These regulations—and the punishments for violating them—applied to everyone equally, including full party members.

The CPK believed children should become self-sufficient at an early age. In many cooperatives, children older than six years had to move away from their parents. They lived in separate boys' and girls' dormitories, where they would grow up alongside the other children of the cooperative. According to Pol Pot's plan, they would spend their mornings learning basic reading and math and their afternoons working in the fields. But in practice, this rarely happened. Many cooperatives had no teachers, since any surviving intellectuals and monks—people with enough education to teach others—had to work in the fields. And often production demands required that children work all day. As children grew older, they moved on to separate boys' and girls' work brigades.

Within each cooperative, people belonged to three categories: members, candidates, and depositees. Members were usually the poor peasants among the base people. Candidates were generally wealthier peasants and poor April 17 people who had been laborers. Depositees were other April 17 people and any people considered class enemies. Though depositees worked alongside everyone else, they weren't considered part of the cooperatives. Work was hard for all, and all suffered during food shortages. But cooperative categories did affect living conditions. Members received better food and got their food first. Depositees had to work hardest and received their food—usually of lower quality—last.

Compared to ordinary citizens, cadre generally had life somewhat easier. They usually had enough food. They also had weapons to ensure their authority. But they too worked long hours and lived communally. Even high-ranking CPK members in Phnom Penh generally ate communally (though they did have plenty of high-quality food), spurned luxury, and remained true to their Communist ideals. The Khmer Rouge did not tolerate the sort of greed and corruption that had plagued earlier Cambodian regimes. (Corrupt officials under Lon Nol had diverted resources to the military and the wealthy, causing widespread starvation. Though even worse starvation happened under Pol Pot, it had other causes.)

The cities stayed empty. Even Phnom Penh was largely a ghost town during Pol Pot's regime. The small area containing the government headquarters and factories was neat and clean. The Khmer Rouge spared some engineers from execution or exile to keep electricity running in this area. Outside it, buildings decayed and cars rusted in the streets. Lawns and marketplaces became farm fields.

In the countryside, living conditions varied considerably. Some zones were naturally more fertile or less devastated by war than others. Also, the government allowed local leaders a lot of independence on issues such as distributing food and punishing wrongdoing.

According to refugees, Democratic Kampuchea contained "good" areas and "bad" areas. In good areas—such as fertile parts of the eastern zone and Battambang Province—people usually had adequate food. In good areas, people could supplement the staples that their cooperatives doled out by tending vegetable gardens, fishing, foraging in the jungle, and trading food with others. Good areas also had few executions. People who lived in these areas said that most of the executions were for crimes for which the death penalty would have applied in earlier times.

Bad areas earned their reputations in two ways. Bad areas typically had unproductive land. In these places, April 17 people did

LABORERS DIG IRRIGATION CANALS BY HAND IN THE COUNTRYSIDE OUTSIDE
Phnom Penh in the mid-1970s.

backbreaking work to clear forests and build irrigation systems, only to create fields that produced poor crops. Bad areas also had rigid rules and numerous executions. For example, in these places seeking supplemental food was a dangerous sign of individualism, and it could bring violent punishment. In bad areas, any accusation by cadre—including children returned from reeducation camps—could lead to execution.

Not all the hundreds of thousands of deaths during Pol Pot's regime resulted from starvation or execution. The Khmer Rouge worked many

"There were 450 children in my youth group, and only one hundred of us survived. Most were killed by the Khmer Rouge or died from starvation or sickness. We got sick often because we didn't have enough food. If the Khmer Rouge took us to the hospital, we were in a worse situation because then we were accused of pretending to be sick, 'feeling sick' they called it, and we were given even less food. The Khmer Rouge used traditional medicine, but it didn't cure any illnesses, and five or six people died in the hospital every day."

—Thavery, a child during the Khmer Rouge revolution

people to death. It forced them to labor in the fields morning to night despite malaria and other serious illnesses. Many people died of untreated disease too. Most of the medicine available consisted of traditional remedies. And medical workers were peasants, not educated professionals. Even when medical centers occasionally used modern treatments, unsterile conditions often led to infection.

All aspects of life in Democratic Kampuchea varied from place to place. And all worsened over time.

MEDIA

The CPK kept absolute control of Democratic Kampuchea partly by eliminating some forms of media and dominating the rest. The party started with radio.

As the Khmer Rouge took over cities, it confiscated all radios and locked them in storage. Only cadre could keep radios. Nevertheless, radio was one of Pol Pot's most important tools. Soon after the Khmer Rouge took the capital, Radio Phnom Penh began broadcasting again, as the mouthpiece of Pol Pot and the CPK. It was the vehicle for Pol Pot's rare public speeches. Its announcers condemned Vietnamese aggression and exaggerated Cambodian victories whenever border struggles flared up. Though cadre were the only Cambodian listeners, they weren't the entire audience. Pol Pot knew that the outside world studied Radio Phnom Penh's broadcasts, and he took advantage of this situation. For instance, in September 1976, the station announced that Pol Pot had resigned as prime minister. He ordered this announcement to confuse his enemies about who really led the country. He was back in office a month later.

The CPK cut off other connections to the outside world soon after April 17, 1975. It ended international telephone, telegraph, and mail services. (The CPK later reestablished connections to a few Communist countries.) It prohibited international travel, except some very limited and tightly controlled travel to China and Vietnam.

Within Democratic Kampuchea, war had already disrupted non-radio communication over long distances. Bombs had destroyed roads and railways. Sabotage and other violence had cut most telephone and telegraph lines. When the CPK reconnected such means of communication, it ensured that all information had to travel via Phnom Penh. Zone headquarters could not communicate directly with one another. Most CPK communication took place by word of mouth, via memos circulated among high-level party leaders, and through memos passed from Phnom Penh to zone administrators. The CPK used messengers—often young radical Communists—to communicate with cadre in other zones. Since cadre had to obey orders from Angkar without question, messengers were very powerful in the outlying areas.

The CPK also tightly controlled print media. The many newspapers that had flourished—and often suffered repression—under earlier Cambodian regimes disappeared. The Khmer Rouge considered it elitist to read anything besides Communist propaganda or CPK documents. Only cadre could spend time reading. Most people had nothing to read. If someone did own or come across a non-Communist text, reading it openly could lead to being declared a class enemy. In many areas, children didn't learn to read or write at all. In these areas, either no one was available to teach the children or they had to spend all their time working. Refugees who escaped Democratic Kampuchea reported not having read any form of news—or even seen a calendar—for more than three years.

FARMERS DANCE IN AN IRRIGATION DITCH WHILE OTHER WORKERS WATCH.
The Khmer Rouge staged such pictures to prove that Cambodian people were happy and prosperous under the new regime.

Cambodian journalism inside Democratic Kampuchea disappeared with the newspapers. The CPK also tried to control international observations of its regime. As it gradually established relations with a few other Communist countries, it allowed some Communist journalists into Democratic Kampuchea. But in general, they reported only stories agreed upon by their home Communist parties and the CPK. Until December 1978, when

The country had no newspapers, and only cadre could keep radios. So how did the CPK spread its propaganda to the average person? It used study and self-criticism sessions. Study sessions consisted of lectures on the Khmer Rouge version of Communism and the work necessary to resurrect Democratic Kampuchea and protect it from enemies. Self-criticism sessions were supposed to improve people by helping them recognize their corrupt, non-Communist thoughts and actions. But instead of improving people, these sessions often increased misery. Self-criticism led easily to accusation and punishment.

SELF-CRITICISM

"[W]e all carry vestiges [traces] of our old class character, deep-rooted for generations, and, after all, the transition to revolutionary proletarian [laboring-class] character is still quite recent. . . . [These vestiges] can be resolved by education, study, criticism and self-criticism, and periodic self-examination of our own revolutionary lifestyle, under the supervision and with the aid of the collective; all this, under the leadership of the Party. It is important to consistently carry out thorough-going educational work, which is aimed at developing collectivist and socialist ownership and

The CPK also held extended study sessions for cadre and youth. Youths often emerged from such sessions as passionate Khmer Rouge supporters. They were ready to denounce their old way of life and all who stood for it, including parents and village elders. Self-criticism sessions strengthened this transformation, encouraging youths to feel publicly ashamed of their parents and their backgrounds.

STATE APPARATUS

Democratic Kampuchea spent nearly a year without a formally defined government structure. Both before and after the constitution took effect, the real power behind the state was a handful of high-ranking CPK members.

From April 1975 to January 1976, when the constitution took effect, Norodom Sihanouk was the nation's figurehead. (He had been the public face of the exile coalition government, the National Union of Kampuchea, and he continued that role after coalition forces—which were mostly Communists by 1975—took over Cambodia.) Under Sihanouk, secret CPK leaders officially directed different areas of government. Pol Pot's area, for instance, consisted of the economy and defense. But the CPK actually governed the country, and Pol Pot controlled the CPK.

In 1976 Democratic Kampuchea held a show election for national assembly members. April 17 people could not vote, and all the candidates were CPK appointees. The new assembly met to approve the constitution, which the CPK leaders had written. The government that this constitution established officially named Pol

Pot prime minister. Other secret CPK leaders filled the remaining top government positions.

Democratic Kampuchea's official government titles had little meaning. The CPK's Central Committee, which determined party policies, actually controlled the government. So what really mattered was one's standing within the CPK. As time went by, even membership in the CPK Central Committee lost some meaning. A small group of the committee's members gradually overshadowed the rest. This group consisted of Pol Pot and his closest associates: Nuon Chea, Vorn Vet, Khieu Samphan, Ieng Sary, and Ieng Thirith.

Loyal supporters enforced the decisions that Pol Pot and his inner circle made. Throughout his regime, Pol Pot ordered violent purges to eliminate people he suspected of working against him—or of not working hard enough to support him. Son Sen, minister of defense, carried out these purges. He commanded not only the military and the national police but also the secret police who rooted out traitors within the CPK. He ultimately controlled Tuol Sleng's S-21 facility, which imprisoned, tortured, and executed accused traitors.

No one was safe from these purges. Even inner-circle Central Committee members were vulnerable. Vorn Vet, for example, was a close associate of Pol Pot and had struggled alongside him for many years. But as Pol Pot grew ever more paranoid, purges reached deeper into the CPK. In 1978 Pol Pot began to suspect that he had lost Vorn Vet's loyalty. Pol Pot had Vorn Vet tortured at S-21. He confessed to working with Vietnam and the CIA, and the Khmer Rouge executed him.

Pol Pot also suspected many zone leaders of disloyalty and often ordered their elimination. Ta Mok, leader of the southwestern zone, carried out many of the zone purges. This role helped him become an important figure in Democratic Kampuchea.

JUSTIFYING VIOLENCE

"We promote broad democracy among the people by a correct application of democratic centralism, so that this immense force will mobilize enthusiastically and rapidly for socialist revolution and construction, at great leaps and bounds forward. . . . On the other hand, we absolutely, without hesitation, apply the dictatorship of the proletariat [working class] to our enemies and to the tiny handful of reactionary [ultraconservative] elements who oppose the revolution, who seek to destroy it, who sell out to the foreign imperialists and reactionaries in order to ruin their own nation, their own people, and their own revolution."

—Pol Pot, 1977

Though the CPK Central Committee's inner circle wielded great power—and used that power brutally—it did not directly cause the terror most Cambodians experienced. Uneducated, inexperienced local authorities were largely responsible for this suffering. Furthermore, cadre and soldiers held a lot of local power, and many of these were only teenagers.

FOREIGN AFFAIRS

Cambodia's Communist movement arose on a tide of opposition to French colonial rule. The movement had swept up Pol

Pot—and many others—when they were students. During this time, Pol Pot developed an extreme sense of nationalism, as well as hostility toward anything he considered imperialist. These sentiments strongly influenced Democratic Kampuchea's foreign affairs. Relations among great world powers—the Soviet Union, the United States, and China—also affected Pol Pot's foreign policy.

Pol Pot's views of foreign countries led him to promote an illusion of complete independence. He claimed that Cambodia's revolution was uniquely Khmer, based on no foreign models, and that Democratic Kampuchea was totally self-sufficient. So when the CPK took control of Cambodia in 1975, the country immediately became isolated. It severed all formal international relations. It even cut potentially beneficial ties.

Democratic Kampuchea did resume diplomatic relations with a few Communist countries. In addition to China, Democratic Kampuchea's most important foreign connection, Democratic Kampuchea resumed relations with Yugoslavia. Pol Pot respected Yugoslavia for staying neutral in the U.S.-Soviet Cold War. He saw both sides in the Cold War as imperialists. The United States interfered in the affairs of smaller countries around the world, such as Vietnam and Cambodia. And the Soviet Union had established a virtual empire in Eastern Europe. (Pol Pot believed that Soviet-supported Vietnam was trying to establish an Indochinese union of Soviet states.) Pol Pot also established relatively close relations with Communist North Korea. He respected North Korean leaders for insisting on self-reliance and consistently opposing the United States.

Though Democratic Kampuchea did deal formally with a few other nations, avoiding enemies dominated its foreign policy. Pol Pot believed that Vietnam and the United States were his key foes. Radio broadcasts and party documents spread this view.

TA MOK *(RIGHT)*, A ZONE LEADER KNOWN FOR RUTHLESS PURGES, GREETS Chinese officials on a diplomatic visit to Cambodia.

They blamed Vietnam and the United States for every Cambodian problem and praised Democratic Kampuchea for defeating these imperialist enemies single-handedly. Pol Pot explained purge after purge by claiming that Vietnam or the United States had tried to overthrow him. Son Sen's police forced thousands of people to confess to spying for Vietnam or the CIA—the gravest crimes in Democratic Kampuchea—and used these confessions to justify killing Pol Pot's political enemies.

Some Cambodian nationalists talked of invading and retaking the Kampuchea Krom region of Vietnam. But Pol Pot was more interested in strengthening his grip on Democratic Kampuchea and realizing the Khmer Communist revolution than in fighting wars of conquest. When border struggles with Vietnam broke out in 1975, he moved quickly to smooth over relations. He knew his country stood little chance of staying independent if bigger, stronger Vietnam chose to invade.

Despite Pol Pot's illusion of self-sufficiency, Democratic Kampuchea could not do without foreign allies. Pol Pot downplayed China's support, but it was crucial to his power and his country's independence. China became Democratic Kampuchea's primary trade partner, selling weapons and buying rice, rubber, and jungle products such as tiger and panther skins, ivory, and ingredients for Chinese medicine. China also provided specialists to help train Cambodian cadre in industry, since most Khmer specialists were dead or doing hard labor in the countryside.

COMMUNIST ADVISERS FROM CHINA POSE WITH CAMBODIAN CADRE AND troops at Angkor Wat in the mid-1970s.

Pol Pot's stance thus opposed the two Cold War superpowers and allied Democratic Kampuchea with China. However, when Vietnam began pressing on the border, China proved unwilling to back an all-out war with Vietnam. Pol Pot had to look for other allies. Hoping to gain U.S. support against Vietnam, he tried to make his regime appear more open and less repressive—even as stories of his brutality drove Americans to revile him. Refugees' reports of human rights abuses in Democratic Kampuchea had even prompted the United Nations Human Rights Commission to inquire about these claims. Several countries also called for more substantive investigations.

By then it was too late for Pol Pot to keep control of Cambodia. A Vietnamese invasion had already begun.

CONCLUSION

THE DEMISE

BY LATE 1978, POL POT'S POLICIES had put Democratic Kampuchea in a precarious position. His anti-Vietnamese stance made an all-out war with Vietnam inevitable. His violent purges had strengthened opposition to him, especially in the eastern zone. And Cambodians reaped no benefits from collectivized agriculture. Instead, they continued to starve despite their hard labor.

INVASION BY VIETNAM

In December 1978, some former Khmer Rouge leaders and eastern zone administrators who had survived the purges met in a Vietnamese-occupied section of the eastern zone. This group included Hun

OF POL POT'S REGIME

SLASHES OF PAINT DEFACE A bust of Pol Pot. As his regime began to crumble, acts of rebellion were more common but still dangerous.

Sen, who had left Democratic Kampuchea the year before, and Heng Samrin. Heng Samrin was an eastern zone military leader who had previously attacked Vietnam during border clashes. During one eastern zone purge, he discovered he was a marked man. He defected to Vietnam with several thousand of his troops. The group and its Vietnamese backers decided that the time was right to overthrow Pol Pot's regime.

Together with Vietnam, this group formed an organization called the Kampuchean United Front for National Salvation (KUFNS). The military forces under KUFNS command were mostly Vietnamese. They consisted of about one hundred thousand Vietnamese soldiers and twenty thousand Cambodian troops. By contrast, the Khmer Rouge faced them with only about sixty thousand soldiers. On December 25, 1978, KUFNS forces invaded Democratic Kampuchea from various points along its border with Vietnam.

Vietnam had originally intended to take only eastern Cambodia. But KUFNS troops met so little resistance in the northeastern and eastern zones that they pressed on. As the Vietnamese advanced, Democratic Kampuchea's agricultural system collapsed. It had already been in poor shape. Not only had the CPK's agricultural policy failed, but natural disasters had caused famine throughout the country. In the Mekong Valley, floods had destroyed crops, while drought had withered much of the rest of the country. Fleeing Khmer Rouge soldiers took what crops and animals they could. When the Khmer Rouge abandoned a cooperative, its April 17 people left too. They had been forced into farming and wanted to go home. As the system unraveled, starving people ate whatever they could find— including livestock and seed rice (rice for the next year's planting).

The leaders of Democratic Kampuchea recognized that they could not repel the invasion. They prepared to leave Phnom Penh. As they did so, Pol Pot met with Norodom Sihanouk and released him from house arrest. Sihanouk agreed to represent Democratic Kampuchea abroad and left for Beijing. Pol Pot left the capital by helicopter for Thailand. Other CPK leaders left by train.

When Vietnamese forces entered Phnom Penh on January 7, 1979, they found it abandoned. On January 8, KUFNS created an interim (temporary) government headed by Heng Samrin. At this

WHEN THE VIETNAMESE TOOK PHNOM PENH IN 1979, THEY FOUND
the unburied bodies of hundreds of executed prisoners at prison camps around the city. Reporters soon spread this evidence of mass murder around the world.

point, the Vietnamese military occupied the entire country. It had pushed the Khmer Rouge troops westward to the Thai border.

INTERNATIONAL REACTIONS

Norodom Sihanouk flew from Beijing to New York to protest the Vietnamese invasion at the United Nations headquarters. He asked the UN to support Pol Pot's regime despite its human rights abuses, citing the danger of letting Vietnam act with such aggression. He won the support of such major anti-Vietnamese, anti-Soviet countries as the United States and China. These countries found expelling the Vietnamese from Democratic Kampuchea so pressing that they even tried to downplay Pol Pot's negative image. They managed to put the investigation of Cambodian genocide cases on hold. (Genocide is mass murder in order to destroy a specific racial, political, or cultural group.)

With such powerful supporters, Democratic Kampuchea's downfall wouldn't be swift. Vietnam's enemies were prepared to ensure that the KUFNS government wouldn't survive. In February 1979, a few weeks after Vietnam invaded Democratic Kampuchea, China retaliated with a two-week attack on northern Vietnam. This attack involved about two hundred thousand Chinese troops. It killed thousands of Chinese and Vietnamese soldiers and destroyed Vietnamese cities near the Chinese border.

PHNOM PENH, 1979

A Soviet diplomat visited Phnom Penh right after the Vietnamese takeover. He was shocked by what he found in the Soviet Embassy. All the windows were broken. One room contained a bloodstain and bullet marks, clear evidence of a shooting. The gardens had become a graveyard stinking of rotting corpses in shallow graves.

THE VIETNAMESE OCCUPATION

Vietnam replaced the interim KUFNS government with a Vietnam-sponsored Cambodian government. The Vietnamese named this new government the People's Republic of Kampuchea (PRK).

The PRK quickly reversed many of Pol Pot's extreme policies. It reintroduced money and marketplaces (places and opportunities for buying and selling). Traditional family relationships could resume, and families could choose to work on their own farms or on collectives. The PRK even allowed some free practice of Buddhism. Although Pol Pot and Ieng Sary had escaped, the PRK tried them in absentia (in absence) and sentenced them to death.

These acts were steps in the right direction, but life in Cambodia remained unsettled and unsatisfactory for many people. Some Cambodians feared the new government, which was still Communist. Others refused to participate in what they considered a Vietnamese colony under a puppet Cambodian government. Furthermore, Vietnamese rule was also harsh. Although the Vietnamese didn't conduct mass executions as the Khmer Rouge had, they nevertheless permitted no opposition. While Vietnamese soldiers occupied Cambodia, they imprisoned more than twenty thousand people for political reasons. One of these prisoners later recalled, "[S]ince I didn't want to work for the government, I was accused of being anti-Vietnamese. . . . I spent one year in a dark cell. They starved us to make us talk. . . . We had showers every ten or fifteen days. . . . Some had broken jaws from being hit; I still carry marks from it."

Pol Pot still commanded a Democratic Kampuchea government in exile on the Thai border. With the political support of the United States, this exile government retained Cambodia's seat at the UN and remained Cambodia's official government in the eyes of many other nations. Furthermore, a deal between China and Thailand allowed the Khmer Rouge to establish bases in Thailand. China also continued to arm the Khmer Rouge in these bases.

Pol Pot wanted to regain control of Cambodia, and he intended to use the hundred thousand Democratic Kampuchea supporters who had also fled to Thailand to do so. The Khmer Rouge sent small groups of soldiers into Cambodia from bases on the Thai border. These guerrilla forces harassed and sabotaged the Vietnamese and terrorized Cambodians who tried to rebuild instead of fighting the Vietnamese. The Khmer Rouge placed land mines in the way of Vietnamese troop movements. It also mined roads and rice paddies to make examples of "unfaithful" Cambodians—those who were farming instead of fighting. This guerrilla war between Pol Pot's supporters and the PRK further destabilized the country.

Because life in Cambodia remained very dangerous, refugee camps in Thailand grew and grew. By late June 1979, more than 250,000 Cambodian refugees were living in Thai camps. These refugees included both Khmer Rouge supporters and people who simply wanted to escape the guerrilla warfare or the harsh occupation.

A CAMBODIAN WOMAN AND HER children take shelter at a refugee camp on the border of Thailand despite flooding there.

Hunger also drove Cambodians to refugee camps. Drought and famine continued. People had eaten most of the seeds intended for replanting. Ongoing violence prevented farming in many areas. In July 1979, the Red Cross and the United Nations Children's Fund (UNICEF) estimated that more than two million Cambodians were in danger of starving. Little of the food sent by other countries reached people inside Cambodia because it traveled via the refugee camps. (Organizations couldn't distribute food directly to the people living in Cambodia because Democratic Kampuchea, not the PRK, held Cambodia's seat in the United Nations.) In the camps along the Thai border, Democratic Kampuchea officials, as representatives of the "legitimate" government of Cambodia, made sure the Khmer Rouge received much of the food to keep their movement alive.

PRK reforms led to better harvests beginning in 1980. But food was still scarce. Since refugees in the Thai camps were getting much more food than the people in Cambodia, even more people fled over the next few years. During the 1980s, more than three hundred thousand non–Khmer Rouge Cambodian refugees spent time in the border camps. The UN began to operate non-Khmer Rouge refugee camps and tried to ensure that aid was directed to these refugees. But the Khmer Rouge diverted that aid by making deals with the Thai military. And the camps served as fertile recruiting grounds for anti-Vietnamese forces such as the Khmer Rouge, Norodom Sihanouk, and former Democrat prime minister Son Sann.

China encouraged Norodom Sihanouk to form a new coalition government with the two other groups recruiting supporters among Cambodian refugees: Democratic Kampuchea and Son Sann's non-Communist group. Khieu Samphan had officially taken over as prime minister of Democratic Kampuchea when Pol Pot officially resigned in December 1979. Sihanouk, Khieu Samphan, and

Son Sann all agreed to form a coalition in 1982. Sihanouk became the nominal leader of the Coalition Government of Democratic Kampuchea (CGDK). This new government stated that it was capitalist and did not oppose religion. The CPK had officially ceased to exist a year earlier. But the same CPK inner circle that had ruled Democratic Kampuchea led the CGDK. Besides the figurehead president, Norodom Sihanouk, and the prime minister, Son Sann, all the CGDK's major positions went to former CPK members. In 1982 the UN recognized the CGDK as Cambodia's official government.

The CGDK commanded about forty thousand troops. Most of these soldiers were Khmer Rouge. They received about one hundred million dollars worth of Chinese weapons throughout the 1980s. In 1982 the CGDK military managed to penetrate some areas of Cambodia. But Vietnamese forces easily pushed the CGDK troops back into Thailand and destroyed their camps. For the next few years, while Vietnamese forces remained in Cambodia, they confined CGDK supporters and troops to Thailand and the border areas.

During this time, Pol Pot and his inner circle—including Son Sen, Ta Mok, Khieu Samphan, and Nuon Chea—continued to recruit and teach classes to young people, whom they hoped would resurrect Democratic Kampuchea. Pol Pot was a popular teacher, just as he had been in the 1950s. One of his students described him as "funny and warm with students." Pol Pot was back in his element. His wife, however, did not fare well. Khieu Ponnary suffered from paranoid schizophrenia (a severe mental illness), and the difficulties of the time overwhelmed her. She moved to a Beijing mental hospital in 1982. In 1985 Pol Pot got married again, to a much younger woman named Mea Son. In the midst of Pol Pot's struggle to regain control of Cambodia, Mea Son gave birth to Pol Pot's daughter, Sith.

WITHDRAWAL OF VIETNAM

Contrary to Pol Pot's beliefs, Vietnam wasn't interested in permanently occupying Cambodia. As the 1980s progressed, Vietnam and other countries took steps to return Cambodia's government fully into Cambodian hands. These events offered Pol Pot a last chance at regaining power.

Continued occupation of Cambodia was growing expensive for Vietnam. It had successfully rebuilt after the Vietnam War, but its Communist policies were causing economic problems. To make matters worse, the United States and China had restricted international trade with Vietnam. Even Vietnam's ally, the Soviet Union, reduced its economic support of Vietnam. The Cold War had been costly, and the Soviet Union's new leader, Mikhail Gorbachev, was trying to improve relations with China and the United States. By 1987 Soviet leaders were encouraging Vietnam to withdraw from Cambodia. Vietnam itself had also begun looking for ways to improve relations with China.

Throughout the 1980s, Vietnam encouraged the PRK to raise and maintain its own army. By 1985 this army numbered about thirty thousand soldiers. These soldiers, assisted by Vietnamese troops, fought to keep CGDK forces on Cambodia's western border.

In 1987 tensions between the two Cambodian governments began to ease. However, the three groups that made up the CGDK had not integrated in spite of their shared exile government. Norodom Sihanouk's supporters and Khmer Rouge forces clashed on the Thai border, and Sihanouk resigned the CGDK presidency. The Soviet Union had been trying to arrange meetings between Sihanouk and Hun Sen, the PRK leader. After Sihanouk quit the Khmer Rouge–dominated CGDK, he agreed to meet with Hun Sen.

Norodom Sihanouk and Hun Sen met in France. They publicly discussed how they could cooperate to end the war and govern Cambodia. The meetings went well at first. Sihanouk and Hun Sen agreed in broad terms to arrange for Vietnam's withdrawal. They also agreed to establish a coalition government in which they would share power. But they couldn't agree on the details, and Sihanouk reconsidered his goals. He returned to the CGDK presidency in 1988.

This backtracking was short-lived, though. Sihanouk became convinced that the Khmer Rouge would resume its human rights abuses if it regained power. So later in 1988, he resigned from the CGDK again and renewed talks with Hun Sen. At various points over the next few years, all four public Cambodian faction leaders—Norodom Sihanouk, Hun Sen, Son Sann, and Khieu Samphan—met to discuss sharing power and ending hostilities. But they never reached a final agreement.

As talks among the Cambodian groups dragged on, China and Vietnam reached an agreement on their involvement in Cambodia. When Vietnam withdrew its troops from Cambodia, China would stop supporting the Khmer Rouge. Vietnam had already lost tens of thousands of soldiers fighting the Khmer Rouge. This deal offered a way to stem Vietnamese casualties while weakening the Khmer Rouge. Vietnam withdrew fifty thousand troops at the end of 1988 and its remaining twenty-six thousand troops in September 1989.

In 1989, between the two Vietnamese troop withdrawals, the government in Phnom Penh made changes to demonstrate its independence from Vietnam. Hun Sen became prime minister of the new State of Cambodia (SOC). The SOC replaced the Vietnam-backed PRK. Cambodia's new government made Buddhism the official state religion, fully reinstituted private property, and allowed trade in real estate.

The same year, Pol Pot claimed to resign from politics. (However, he seems to have remained the Khmer Rouge's real leader.) As usual, he was trying to obscure the Khmer Rouge power structure. This time he was also reacting to his own bad reputation. In Cambodia and around the world, Pol Pot's name had become synonymous with the horrors of his regime. And he couldn't ignore the popularity of subsequent reforms in Cambodia. The United States and China still ensured that the Khmer Rouge–dominated CGDK represented Cambodia in the UN. They also blocked arrests and trials for Khmer Rouge human rights violations. Furthermore, the United States kept sending aid only to the Khmer Rouge–dominated refugee camps. But movements were under way in the U.S. Congress to condemn the Khmer Rouge and stop supporting them. Pol Pot knew that his name was a liability to the Khmer Rouge. He withdrew it to further the Khmer Rouge's cause.

Vietnam's 1989 departure gave the Khmer Rouge the opportunity it had been waiting for. It seized some Cambodian territories, including lands rich in natural resources such as gemstones and timber. It sold these resources in Thailand for money to buy weapons. By 1990 Khmer Rouge–led resistance forces controlled Cambodia's mountainous northwestern and southwestern regions. They seemed prepared to move on the port city of Kampong Som and the city of Battambang.

The four Cambodian factions couldn't—or wouldn't—end hostilities on their own. So the United Nations Security Council's permanent members (the United States, the United Kingdom, France, the Soviet Union, and China) stepped in. They tried to work out a UN solution to Cambodia's problems. These negotiations resulted in the Paris Agreement of October 1991. The Paris Agreement in turn established the United Nations Transitional Authority in Cambodia (UNTAC). UNTAC would keep the peace and prepare the country for national elections.

AS THE KHMER ROUGE WITHDREW FROM ITS STRONGHOLDS, CAMBODIANS searched for evidence of missing loved ones. During the 1980s and 1990s, they excavated some of the mass graves *(above)*, known as the Killing Fields, and built memorials to the victims buried there.

The Khmer Rouge took advantage of this opportunity for a return to politics within Cambodia. But it refused to disarm or disband its army. The Khmer Rouge continued using its military forces to control the areas it had seized after Vietnam's withdrawal.

Despite the Khmer Rouge's belligerence, UNTAC conducted elections on May 23, 1993. These elections produced a coalition government in which Norodom Sihanouk's party and Hun Sen's party shared power. The new government crowned Sihanouk king again. It renamed the country the Kingdom of Cambodia.

In 1994 the Cambodian national assembly banned the Khmer Rouge. The Cambodian military began to attack the Khmer Rouge. And the United States finally completed a policy change that had been in the works since the 1980s. The U.S. Congress passed the Cambodian Genocide Justice Act, which made efforts to punish those responsible for Cambodia's genocide official U.S. policy.

In the Khmer Rouge's territories, it tried to reestablish 1970s conditions. It attempted collectivization, tried to ban Buddhism, and prepared for a long war to oust foreign control. (The Khmer Rouge still considered Cambodia's government to be Vietnamese puppets.) But the recent reforms were too popular, and Cambodians were sick of war. Even devoted Khmer Rouge supporters began to abandon the Khmer Rouge movement.

THE DEMISE OF POL POT

In 1994 Pol Pot, Khieu Samphan, Ta Mok, Nuon Chea, and Son Sen still led the Khmer Rouge. In 1995 Pol Pot suffered a stroke that left him partly paralyzed. Ta Mok rose to head the inner circle. He took over most of the everyday leadership functions of the Khmer Rouge, even though Pol Pot remained in charge. But just as the Khmer Rouge's lower ranks were fragmenting, so was its leadership. In August 1996, Ieng Sary defected to the Kingdom of Cambodia. In return, he received a pardon for the crime of genocide (of which the PRK had found him guilty in 1979) and for participating in the Khmer Rouge after its prohibition in 1994. Thousands of other Khmer Rouge soldiers and civilians soon abandoned the cause too.

As the movement crumpled, Pol Pot accused Ta Mok, Nuon Chea, and Son Sen of working with Vietnam. He had Khmer Rouge soldiers arrest all three men. The movement then split. Some of the remaining Khmer Rouge stayed loyal to Pol Pot. The rest sided with Ta Mok. In response to the split, Pol Pot ordered his people to murder about twenty of Ta Mok's supporters and burn down the houses of others.

On June 9, 1997, Pol Pot had Son Sen and his family murdered. This act caused most of Pol Pot's remaining supporters to abandon him. Ta Mok's people set out to arrest him. With his family and a few loyal Khmer Rouge members, he fled through the jungle. Pol Pot's paralysis made for slow going, and Ta Mok's forces caught up on June 16. They staged a show trial for the murders of Son Sen and the others and for the destruction Pol Pot had ordered the week before.

Ta Mok kept Pol Pot under house arrest in his jungle camp. Meanwhile, Pol Pot's health continued to deteriorate.

During his imprisonment, Pol Pot at last spoke publicly about the charges of genocide and terror placed against him. Even at the end of his life, he claimed that he had never intended bloodshed and meant only to struggle for the good of his country. He insisted the killings were simply historical inevitabilities or mistakes made in the course of revolution. "I would like to tell you that I came to carry out the struggle, not to kill people," he said. "Even now, and you can look at me, am I a savage person? My conscience is clear."

As Pol Pot languished in the jungle, a group of foreign coun-

POL POT SPOKE TO REPORTERS
at his jungle camp in 1998.

THE CAMBODIA TRIBUNAL

Pol Pot died before the world could bring him to justice. But some other Khmer Rouge leaders still await trial for war crimes and crimes against humanity. The trials were delayed for a decade by disagreement between the Cambodian government and the UN on how to conduct them and by fear of reigniting civil war. In 2007 Cambodian authorities finally arrested several surviving Khmer Rouge leaders. In 2008 Ieng Sary, Ieng Thirith, Khieu Samphan, Nuon Chea, and Kaing Kek Ieu (Son Sen's subordinate who oversaw S-21) wait in a Phnom Penh prison for trial by the Cambodia Tribunal, a court of Cambodian and foreign judges.

tries, including the United States, was arranging to try Pol Pot and other surviving Khmer Rouge leaders for crimes against humanity. On the night of April 15, 1998, Pol Pot heard that Ta Mok's group intended to release him to this international tribunal. Pol Pot went to bed even weaker than usual. He died of a heart attack around 10:15 P.M., with Mea Song and Sith beside him.

The remaining Khmer Rouge leaders surrendered in 1999. But Cambodia is still struggling to recover from the damage it suffered under Pol Pot's brutal regime.

WHO'S WHO?

HUN SEN (B. 1952): Hun Sen was born into a peasant family. He dropped out of school and fought with the Khmer Rouge for seven years. In 1977 he learned that the party planned to purge him, and he fled to Vietnam. There he joined other Cambodian refugees whom Vietnam was grooming to overthrow Pol Pot. When Vietnam invaded Democratic Kampuchea in 1979, Hun Sen rose to the top of Cambodia's new government. He has been prime minister of Cambodia since 1985.

IENG SARY (B. 1925): Ieng Sary was born to a Chinese-Khmer family in Kampuchea Krom. As a child, he left Vietnam to live with relatives in Cambodia. He attended the Sisowath School in Phnom Penh, where he displayed academic brilliance and a strong interest in politics. He continued his education at the Paris Institute of Political Studies in the 1950s. While in Paris, he joined the Marxist Circle and married fellow radical Khieu Thirith. After returning to Cambodia, he rose through its Communist Party ranks and became a member of its inner circle. When the Khmer Rouge seized Phnom Penh in 1975, Ieng Sary became Democratic Kampuchea's deputy prime minister and foreign minister. After Vietnam invaded Democratic Kampuchea in 1979, Ieng Sary continued his work with the Khmer Rouge in their headquarters on the Thai border. In 1996 he defected to Hun Sen's government. He was arrested and imprisoned in 2007. He awaits trial in Phnom Penh for war crimes and crimes against humanity.

IENG THIRITH (B. 1932): Ieng Thirith (born Khieu Thirith) belonged to an intellectual family. She was the first Cambodian woman to receive a degree in English literature. She and her older sister, Khieu Ponnary, met many future political activists when they attended the Sisowath School. Like several of their peers, the sisters continued their education in Paris and joined the Marxist Circle. Khieu Thirith married Ieng Sary in 1951 and changed her name to Ieng Thirith. When they returned to Cambodia, she taught school and used her salary to support Communist newspapers. A member of Pol Pot's inner circle, she became minister for social affairs in

Democratic Kampuchea. When Vietnam invaded in 1979, she fled Phnom Penh with her husband and Pol Pot. She is currently imprisoned in Phnom Penh, awaiting trial for crimes against humanity and war crimes.

KHIEU PONNARY (1920–2003): Khieu Ponnary, older sister of Khieu Thirith, was also an intellectual. Khieu Ponnary was the first Cambodian woman to receive a baccalaureate degree, from the Sisowath School. She continued her education in Paris and joined the Marxist Circle there. After returning to Phnom Penh, she taught high school and married Saloth Sar. Though she worked with her husband and her sister in the Communist movement, she did not rise within the party ranks. After the Vietnamese invasion in 1979, she separated from her husband, who was trying to revive his revolution on the Thai border. She sought treatment for mental illness in Beijing. Then she returned to Cambodia and lived with her sister and Ieng Sary until her death.

KHIEU SAMPHAN (B. 1931): Khieu Samphan was one of the most intellectual Khmer Rouge leaders. He attended the Sisowath School in Phnom Penh, then earned a PhD in economics at the University of Paris. After returning to Phnom Penh in 1959, he taught law, published a journal, and won a seat in Cambodia's national assembly. He also worked briefly in Norodom Sihanouk's cabinet before Lon Nol's coup in 1970. After the Communists took power in 1975, he became president of Democratic Kampuchea's state presidium. He awaits trial in Phnom Penh on charges of war crimes and crimes against humanity.

LON NOL (1913–1985): Lon Nol was born into a Cambodian peasant family. A career soldier, he steadily rose through the ranks to lead Norodom Sihanouk's police and military. In 1970, with U.S. support, he and Prince Sisowath Sirik Matak seized control of Cambodia's government while Sihanouk was out of the country. Corruption plagued Lon Nol's regime. He gradually lost public support as Khmer Rouge forces took over the country. In 1975, shortly before the Khmer Rouge took Phnom Penh, he evacuated. Lon Nol eventually settled in the United States. He died of heart failure in Fullerton, California.

NORODOM SIHANOUK (B. 1922): Norodom Sihanouk was born to the daughter and son-in-law of King Sisowath Monivong. French authorities chose Sihanouk for the throne in 1941. He soon began pursuing independence from France and won it in 1953. In 1955 he gave up the throne to his father in order to participate in national elections. He led Cambodia's government until Lon Nol overthrew him in 1970. While Sihanouk lived in exile in Beijing, he joined a coalition with Cambodia's Communists, who were fighting to overthrow Lon Nol. When the Communists took Phnom Penh in 1975, Sihanouk returned as a figurehead leader of Cambodia. He soon gave up his position and spent the remaining Democratic Kampuchea years under house arrest. When Vietnam invaded Cambodia in 1979, he began to act as the Khmer Rouge's spokesman abroad. After Vietnam withdrew and elections established a new government in 1993, Sihanouk became king again. In 2004 he stepped down, to be replaced by his son Norodom Sihamoni.

NUON CHEA (B. 1927): Nuon Chea was born Lau Ben Kon into a wealthy Chinese-Khmer family. He joined the Thai Communist Party while living in Bangkok, Thailand, where he attended university and law school. He joined the Cambodian Communists in 1951 and later worked with Saloth Sar in Phnom Penh. Nuon Chea's standing in the party steadily increased over time, but Saloth Sar eventually overtook him for the number one position. As Democratic Kampuchea's national assembly president, he was the regime's second in command and became known as Brother Number Two. He continued to work with the Khmer Rouge on the Thai border after Vietnam occupied Cambodia in 1979. He awaits trial in Phnom Penh for crimes against humanity and war crimes.

POL POT (1925 OR 1928–1998): Pol Pot was born Saloth Sar into a wealthy Khmer farm family with royal connections. He became a Communist while studying in Paris in the 1950s. When he returned to Cambodia, he joined its underground Communist movement. He rose to lead the Communist Party of Kampuchea and later assumed the name Pol Pot.

(He was also known as Brother Number One.) When Communist Khmer Rouge forces took Phnom Penh in 1975, he became the leader of all Cambodia and Democratic Kampuchea's official prime minister. After Vietnam invaded Cambodia in 1979, Pol Pot continued to gather supporters in Cambodian refugee camps along the Thai border. He led the Khmer Rouge until it split in 1997 and Ta Mok arrested him. He died of a heart attack in Ta Mok's custody.

SON SEN (1930–1997): Like most of the Khmer Rouge's top leaders, Son Sen went to school in Phnom Penh and then studied in Paris in the 1950s, where he joined the Marxist Circle. After returning to Cambodia, he and his wife Yun Yat taught at the Sisowath School. Meanwhile, he worked with the Communists in Phnom Penh. He quit teaching in 1963. He rose to the party's Central Committee and became Democratic Kampuchea's minister of defense. He commanded not only the military but also the secret police. When the Vietnamese took Phnom Penh, Son Sen joined the other Khmer Rouge leaders on the Thai border. In the 1990s, he supported negotiating peace with the government in Phnom Penh. As a result, he fell out of favor with Pol Pot. In 1997 Pol Pot had Son Sen and his family killed for supposedly communicating with Pol Pot's Vietnamese enemies. This act turned most of the remaining Khmer Rouge against Pol Pot.

TA MOK (1926–2006): Ta Mok was born Chhit Choeun into a wealthy Chinese-Khmer farming family. He joined Cambodia's Communists by way of the anti-French resistance movement. He rose to command the southwestern zone during Cambodia's civil war between the Khmer Rouge and Lon Nol's government (1970–1975). He gained even more military and political power during the Democratic Kampuchea years (1975–1979). After Vietnam invaded Cambodia in 1979, Ta Mok continued as a Khmer Rouge leader at its headquarters on the Thai border. When the Khmer Rouge split in 1997, he apprehended Pol Pot and kept him under house arrest until his death in 1998. In 1999 the Cambodian army arrested Ta Mok in Thailand for participating in the outlawed Khmer Rouge. He spent the rest of his life imprisoned in Phnom Penh. He died of tuberculosis before his war crimes trial.

TIMELINE

802 Jayavaraman II becomes god-king of Cambodia, marking the beginning of the Angkor period.

1431 A Thai army captures Angkor, marking the end of the Angkor period.

1863 Cambodia becomes a French protectorate.

1925 OR 1928 Saloth Sar is born on May 19.

1939–1945 In World War II, the Axis powers (Germany, Italy, and Japan) fight the Allied nations (including the United Kingdom, the United States, the Soviet Union, and China).

1941 Norodom Sihanouk becomes king of Cambodia in April.

1942 On July 20, a demonstration organized by nationalist leader Son Ngoc Thanh marches on the Cambodian royal palace in Phnom Penh. French officials arrest some nationalist leaders. Others flee to the countryside. The nationalist movement splits into Communist and non-Communist groups.

1946 The First Indochina War, which lasts until 1954, begins. In this war, France fights to regain control of Vietnam, which Vietnamese Communist leader Ho Chi Minh has declared independent. Thailand returns Cambodian territory seized in 1941.

1949–1953 Saloth Sar studies in France and joins the French Communist Party.

1951 Cambodian nationalists form a rival government with Communist Son Ngoc Minh as its president. Cambodian Communists form the Khmer People's Revolutionary Party (KPRP), which is separate from—but still directed by—the Indochinese Communist Party (ICP).

1953 Saloth Sar returns to Cambodia after losing his French scholarship. He works with Cambodian and Vietnamese Communists in the countryside of both nations. Norodom Sihanouk campaigns for Cambodia's independence from France. In November France grants Cambodia independence.

1954 An international conference in Geneva, Switzerland, divides Vietnam into a Communist North Vietnam and a non-Communist South Vietnam. The Geneva Conference also recognizes Sihanouk's government—not the Communist-led resistance government—as Cambodia's legitimate government. Half of Cambodia's Communists flee to North Vietnam, while the rest go into hiding in Cambodia. Saloth Sar moves to Phnom Penh to do political work.

1955–1959 Following a secret deal between Norodom Sihanouk and Cambodian Communist leader Sieu Heng, Sihanouk's police eliminate most of the Communist leaders in the Cambodian countryside.

1956 Saloth Sar and Khieu Ponnary marry in Phnom Penh.

1963 Students in Siem Reap riot against Sihanouk. The Cambodian Communist Party—now called the Worker's Party of Kampuchea (WPK)—holds a Party Congress confirming Saloth Sar as party secretary. Saloth Sar and Ieng Sary leave Phnom Penh to organize Communist resistance in the countryside.

1967 Rebels in Samlaut kill two government solders in protest of General Lon Nol's rice collection scheme. The government cracks down heavily on suspected rebels and Communists.

1969 Khmer Rouge antigovernment military offensives begin. The United States bombs Cambodia to hamper Vietnamese Communist war efforts.

1970 On March 18, Lon Nol and Sisowath Sirik Matak over-throw Norodom Sihanouk. Sihanouk allies with Cambodian Communists to form an exile government and a military National Unified Front to oppose Lon Nol's government. From April to June, South Vietnam and the United States invade Cambodia searching for the South Vietnamese Communist command center.

1970–1975 The National Unified Front and Vietnamese Communist forces launch yearly offensives against Lon Nol's forces.

1973 The U.S. Congress halts U.S. bombing of Cambodia.

1975 On April 17, Khmer Rouge soldiers take Phnom Penh. On April 30, the Vietnam War ends with a Communist victory.

1976 In January the Constitution of Democratic Kampuchea takes effect, and Pol Pot officially becomes prime minister.

1976–1978 Pol Pot begins to purge "enemies" from the party—now called the Communist Party of Kampuchea (CPK)—and from the larger society. Hunger and overwork increase in farming collectives. Border skirmishes between Vietnamese and Cambodian forces occur.

1977 In September Pol Pot gives a radio speech announcing the existence of the CPK and that he heads it. In December Vietnam invades Cambodia, seizes hostages, and withdraws.

1978 In December Khmer Rouge defectors and other Cambodians in a Vietnam-controlled border area form the Vietnam-backed Kampuchean United Front for National Salvation (KUFNS) to overthrow Pol Pot's government.

1979 In January Vietnamese forces occupy Phnom Penh. KUFNS forms a new government led by Heng Samrin. In December Pol Pot steps down as prime minister of Democratic Kampuchea. Khieu Samphan becomes the regime's public leader.

1982 Norodom Sihanouk, Son Sann, and Pol Pot join forces to form the Coalition Government of Democratic Kampuchea (CGDK) in exile.

1988–1989 Vietnam withdraws its troops from Cambodia. The government in Phnom Penh, led by Hun Sen, renames the country the State of Cambodia.

1993 The United Nations Transitional Authority in Cambodia holds elections. Norodom Sihanouk's party and Hun Sen's party share power. The new government renames the country the Kingdom of Cambodia.

1994 The Cambodian government bans the Khmer Rouge.

1997 Pol Pot orders the murder of Khmer Rouge leader Son Sen and his family. Ta Mok's Khmer Rouge faction arrests Pol Pot and tries him for the murders.

1998 Pol Pot dies of a heart attack on April 15 while imprisoned by Ta Mok's group.

1999 The remains of the Khmer Rouge movement dissolves.

2007 Several surviving Khmer Rouge leaders, including Ieng Sary and Ieng Thirith, are arrested and imprisoned.

2008 Ieng Sary and other Khmer Rouge leaders await trial for war crimes and crimes against humanity.

GLOSSARY

Angkar: the Organization; the name Angkar referred to the secret leadership of Cambodia's Communist revolutionary government prior to the establishment of Democratic Kampuchea in 1976. At first Angkar meant the Communist Party's Central Committee. By 1975 it referred mostly to Pol Pot and Nuon Chea.

April 17 people: people evacuated from Cambodian cities after the Khmer Rouge won the Cambodian civil war on April 17, 1975

base people: people who lived in the countryside before the Khmer Rouge evacuated Cambodia's cities

cadre: a person or people trained by the Communist Party to promote and enforce Communist ideology

capitalism: an economic system characterized by private ownership of property and by prices determined in free markets

capitalist: someone who invests money into a business for the purpose of making more money

coalition: a temporary alliance of different political parties or governments to achieve a common goal

collectivize: to reorganize society into collectives. In a collective, a group of people work together for the benefit of the collective and the nation rather than for personal gain. Communist authorities govern all aspects of life in a collectivized society.

Communist: someone who favors community ownership of all property. Communists support armed revolution and collectivization as a means of redistributing wealth more fairly.

conservative: opposed to broad changes in society and to restricting free-market economic systems

democratic: governed by the people through free elections

exile government: a government composed of leaders living outside their home country. An exile government opposes the government in power at home.

front: a temporary alliance of diverse groups to achieve a common goal

guerrilla force: a military group fighting against formal government troops, typically using harassment, sabotage, and terror

imperialist: someone who favors gaining control of other countries

Issarak: "independence" in the Khmer language; a group or individual struggling for Cambodian independence from France

Khmer Rouge: red Khmer; Cambodian Communists and their supporters under Pol Pot

the left: people who support broad societal changes to improve the lives of the common people; liberals

Marxist Circle: the quasi-Communist reading and discussion group that Saloth Sar, Ieng Sary, and other important Cambodian Communist leaders attended while studying in Paris

national assembly: a legislative body made up of elected representatives

nationalism: devotion to one's nation and desire for national independence

purge: to remove undesirable members. In the Khmer Rouge, purging often meant execution.

the right: people who oppose broad changes in society; conservatives

Socialism: a system in which groups of workers or the nation as a whole, not individuals, own the means of production

Soviet Union: the Union of Soviet Socialist Republics (USSR), a country in Eastern Europe and northern Asia from 1922–1991, made up of Russia and fourteen other Communist republics

SOURCE NOTES

16 Pol Pot, "Interview of
    Comrade POL POT Secretary
    of the Central Committee
    of the Communist Party of
    Kampuchea Prime Minister of
    the Government of Democratic
    Kampuchea to the Delegation
    of Yugoslav Journalists in a Visit
    to Democratic Kampuchea,
    March 17, 1978," (Department
    of Press and Information,
    Ministry of Foreign Affairs,
    Democratic Kampuchea), 20.

16 Pol Pot to North Korean pub-
    lic, October 4, 1977, quoted
    in Ben Kiernan, *How Pol Pot
    Came to Power: Colonialism,
    Nationalism, and Communism
    in Cambodia, 1930–1975* (New
    Haven, CT: Yale University
    Press, 2004), 38.

21 David P. Chandler, *Brother
    Number One: A Political
    Biography of Pol Pot* (Boulder,
    CO: Westview Press, 1999), 7.

29 Ben Kiernan, *The Pol Pot
    Regime: Race, Power, and
    Genocide in Cambodia
    under the Khmer Rouge,
    1975–79* (New Haven, CT: Yale

University Press, 2002), 11.

42 Pol Pot, "Long Live the 17th
    Anniversary of the Communist
    Party of Kampuchea,"
    September 19, 1977, (unof-
    ficial translation by Group
    of Kampuchean Residents in
    America), 22.

43 Soth Polin to David Chandler,
    October 1988 and November
    1989, quoted in Chandler,
    Brother Number One, 52.

46 Pol Pot, "Long Live the 17th
    Anniversary of the Communist
    Party of Kampuchea," 23.

54 Ibid., 38.

55 Ibid., 39.

65 Richard Nixon, *Public
    Papers of the Presidents of
    the United States: Richard
    Nixon; Containing the Public
    Messages, Speeches, and
    Statements of the President:
    1970: Book I—January 1 to July
    17, 1975* (Washington, DC:
    Government Printing Office,
    1971), 549.

69 Thomas Blanton and William

Burr, eds., "Recorded
Conversation between Mr.
Kissinger and the President,
December 9, 1970, 8:45 p.m.,"
*The Kissinger Telecons: National
Security Archive Electronic
Briefing Book No. 123*, May 26,
2004, http://www.gwu.edu/
~nsarchiv/NSAEBB/NSAEBB123/
Box%2029,%20File%202,%
20Kissinger%20%96%20
President%20Dec%209,%20
1970%208,45%20pm%20%200.
pdf (September 1, 2007).

74 Pre Veng Province Committee
to provincial cadre, April 1974,
quoted in David Chandler, *The
Tragedy of Cambodian History:
Politics, War, and Revolution
Since 1945* (New Haven, CT:
Yale University Press, 1991),
231.

76 Hoeung Hing Kim to David
Chandler, January 1989, quot-
ed in Chandler, *The Tragedy of
Cambodian History*, 243.

77 Gerald R. Ford, *Public
Papers of the Presidents of
the United States: Gerald R.
Ford; Containing the Public
Messages, Speeches, and
Statements of the President:
1975: Book I—January 1 to July

17, 1975* (Washington, DC:
Government Printing Office,
1977), 279–280.

77 Gerald R. Ford, *Public
Papers of the Presidents of
the United States: Gerald R.
Ford; Containing the Public
Messages, Speeches, and
Statements of the President:
1974* (Washington, DC:
Government Printing Office,
1975), 779.

78 Pol Pot, "Long Live the 17th
Anniversary of the Communist
Party of Kampuchea," 71.

79 Voice of the National United
Front of Cambodia to the people of Phnom Penh, April 16,
1975, quoted in Kiernan, *The
Pol Pot Regime*, 31.

79 Pol Pot, "Long Live the 17th
Anniversary of the Communist
Party of Kampuchea," 48.

80 Pol Pot, "Interview of Comrade
POL POT," 5.

82 Loung Ung, *First They Killed
My Father: A Daughter of
Cambodia Remembers* (New
York: HarperCollins, 2000), 17.

88 Aun to Carol Wagner, 1994,
quoted in Carol Wagner, *Soul*

*Survivors: Stories of Women
and Children in Cambodia,*
(Berkeley, CA: Creative Arts
Book Company, 2002), 128.

90 Pol Pot, "Interview of Comrade
POL POT," 4.

91 Marie Alexandrine Martin,
Cambodia: A Shattered Society
(Berkeley: University of
California Press, 1994), 194.

94 Pol Pot, "Interview of Comrade
POL POT," 5.

97 Pol Pot to Communist Party
cadre, December 1976, quoted
in Chandler, *Brother Number
One*, 129.

97 Elizabeth Becker, *When the
War Was Over: Cambodia and
the Khmer Rouge Revolution*
(New York: PublicAffairs, 1998),
236.

99 Pol Pot, "Interview of Comrade
POL POT," 2.

100 Pol Pot to the people of
Cambodia, September 1978,
quoted in Becker, *When the
War Was Over*, 185.

100 Pol Pot, "Interview of Comrade
POL POT," 12.

100 Kiernan, *The Pol Pot Regime*,
239.

101 Pol Pot, "Long Live the 17th
Anniversary of the Communist
Party of Kampuchea," 10.

103 Chandler, *Brother Number
One*, 151.

104 Kiernan, *The Pol Pot Regime*,
425.

112 Wagner, *Soul Survivors*, 193.

116 Pol Pot, "Long Live the 17th
Anniversary of the Communist
Party of Kampuchea," 57.

119 Ibid., 62.

129 Martin, *Cambodia: A Shattered
Society*, 226.

132 Chandler, *Brother Number
One*, 175.

138 Ibid., 183.

SELECTED BIBLIOGRAPHY

Becker, Elizabeth. *When the War Was Over: Cambodia and the Khmer Rouge Revolution.* New York: PublicAffairs, 1998.

Blanton, Thomas, and William Burr, eds. *The Kissinger Telecons: National Security Archive Electronic Briefing Book No. 123.* May 26, 2004. http://www.gwu.edu/~nsarchiv/NSAEBB/NSAEBB123 (September 1, 2007).

Chandler, David P. *Brother Number One: A Political Biography of Pol Pot.* Boulder, CO: Westview Press, 1999.

———. *A History of Cambodia.* Boulder, CO: Westview Press, 1992.

———. *The Tragedy of Cambodian History: Politics, War, and Revolution Since 1945.* New Haven, CT: Yale University Press, 1991.

Dith Pran, comp. *Children of Cambodia's Killing Fields: Memoirs by Survivors.* Edited by Kim DePaul. New Haven, CT: Yale University Press, 1997.

Ford, Gerald R. *Public Papers of the Presidents of the United States: Gerald R. Ford; Containing the Public Messages, Speeches, and Statements of the President: 1974.* Washington, DC: Government Printing Office, 1975.

———. *Public Papers of the Presidents of the United States: Gerald R. Ford; Containing the Public Messages, Speeches, and Statements of the President: 1975.* Book I—January 1 to July 17, 1975. Washington, DC: Government Printing Office, 1977.

Hsu, Immanuel C. Y. *The Rise of Modern China.* New York: Oxford University Press, 1990.

Jackson, Karl D., ed. *Cambodia 1975–1978: Rendezvous with Death.* Princeton, NJ: Princeton University Press, 1989.

Kiernan, Ben. *How Pol Pot Came to Power: Colonialism, Nationalism, and Communism in Cambodia, 1930–1975.* New Haven, CT: Yale University Press, 2004.

———. *The Pol Pot Regime: Race, Power, and Genocide in Cambodia under the Khmer Rouge, 1975–79.* New Haven, CT: Yale University Press, 2002.

———, ed. *Genocide and Democracy in Cambodia: The Khmer Rouge, the United Nations, and the International Community.* New Haven, CT: Yale University Southeast Asia Studies, 1993. Loung Ung. *First They Killed My Father: A Daughter of Cambodia Remembers.* New York: Harper-Collins, 2000.

Martin, Marie Alexandrine. *Cambodia: A Shattered Society.* Translated by Mark W. McLeod. Berkeley: University of California Press, 1994.

Nixon, Richard. *Public Papers of the Presidents of the United States: Richard Nixon; Containing the Public Messages, Speeches, and Statements of the President: 1970. Book I—January 1 to July 17, 1975.* Washington, DC: Government Printing Office, 1971.

Pol Pot. "Interview of Comrade POL POT Secretary of the Central Committee of the Communist Party of Kampuchea Prime Minister of the Government of Democratic Kampuchea to the Delegation of Yugoslav Journalists in a Visit to Democratic Kampuchea, March 17, 1978." Phnom Penh: Department of Press and Information, Ministry of Foreign Affairs, Democratic Kampuchea.

———. "Long Live the 17th Anniversary of the Communist Party of Kampuchea," speech given on September 19, 1977. Translated by the Group of Kampuchean Residents in America, New York.

Ponchaud, François. *Cambodia: Year Zero.* Translated by Nancy Amphoux. New York: Holt, Rinehart, and Winston, 1978.

Vickery, Michael. *Cambodia 1975–1982.* Chiang Mai, Thailand: Silkworm Books, 1999.

Wagner, Carol. *Soul Survivors: Stories of Women and Children in Cambodia.* Berkeley, CA: Creative Arts Book Company, 2002.

FURTHER READING AND WEBSITES

BOOKS

Dith Pran, comp., and Kim DePaul, ed. *Children of Cambodia's Killing Fields: Memoirs by Survivors.* New Haven, CT: Yale University Press, 1997. This anthology offers recollections by adult survivors of childhoods lived under the Khmer Rouge.

Gay, Kathlyn. *Mao Zedong's China.* Minneapolis: Twenty-First Century Books, 2008. This young adult book offers a very readable history of China's Communist revolution.

Goldstein, Margaret J. *Cambodia in Pictures.* Minneapolis: Twenty-First Century Books, 2004. This young-adult book provides an overview of the land, history, government, people, cultural life, and economy of Cambodia.

Haing Ngor and Roger Warner. *A Cambodian Odyssey.* New York: Macmillan Publishing Company, 1987. This book describes the experiences of a Cambodian doctor who survived Pol Pot's Cambodia in labor camps by lying about his background.

Levy, Debbie. *The Vietnam War.* Minneapolis: Twenty-First Century Books, 2004. This book describes the United States' efforts to curb the spread of Communism in Vietnam.

Loung Ung. *Lucky Child: A Daughter of Cambodia Reunites with the Sister She Left Behind.* New York: HarperCollins, 2005. In this book, Loung Ung describes growing up as a Cambodian refugee in the United States and revisiting Cambodia more than a decade after the fall of Democratic Kampuchea.

Someth May. *Cambodian Witness: The Autobiography of Someth May.* New York: Random House, 1986. Author Someth May recounts his childhood in Cambodia before the Khmer Rouge came to power and his experiences lying about his background and surviving the Pol Pot years.

WEBSITES

Cambodian Genocide Program
> http://www.yale.edu/cgp
> This is the official website for the Cambodian Genocide Program
> at Yale University. It provides links to information about the Khmer
> Rouge atrocities and the Cambodia Tribunal.

Cambodian Recent History and Contemporary Society: An Introductory
Course
> http://www.seasite.niu.edu/khmer/Ledgerwood/Contents.htm
> On this website, Northern Illinois University anthropology professor
> Judy Ledgerwood gives a neatly organized and very informative intro-
> ductory course on Cambodian history, from 1975 to the present.

Cambodia Tribunal Monitor
> http://www.cambodiatribunal.org
> This site provides updated news on the Cambodia Tribunal's activities,
> as well as expert commentary and video webcasts as the trials unfold.

Documentation Center of Cambodia
> http://www.dccam.org
> This website documents the human rights abuses that took place un-
> der the Khmer Rouge. It offers a huge archive of texts, photos, videos,
> music, and other documents, including many survivors' stories.

Human Rights Watch: Cambodia
> http://www.hrw.org/doc?t=asia&c=cambod
> Human Rights Watch is an organization dedicated to investigating and
> stopping human rights violations around the world. Its Cambodia Web
> page provides news, commentary, and other information on Cambo-
> dian human rights issues of the past and present.

Khmer Rouge Trial Task Force

http://www.cambodia.gov.kh/krt/english/index.htm
This Cambodian government website offers details on the establishment
and proceedings of the Cambodia Tribunal.

Their Majesties Norodom Sihanouk and Norodom Monineath Sihanouk

http://www.norodomsihanouk.info
This is former king Norodom Sihanouk's personal website. It provides
insights into the Cambodian royal family, as well as a link to the personal website of Cambodia's reigning king, Norodom Sihamoni.

Visual Geography Series: Cambodia

http://www.vgsbooks.com
Visit vgsbooks.com, the home page of the Visual Geography Series®,
and click on Cambodia for useful online information, including the
latest on the war crime trials of Khmer Rouge leaders. Link to geo-
graphical, historical, demographic, cultural, and economic websites.

Welcome to the Kingdom of Cambodia

http://www.cambodia.gov.kh/unisql1/egov/english/home.view.html
This is the English version of Cambodia's official government website.
Among many other things, it gives information about current political
events in Cambodia.

INDEX

Phnom Penh, 6–8, 76–80, 81, 82–83; trials of, 139, 140–141
Killing Fields, 136

Lon Nol, 6, 51, 53, 55, 58, 69, 77–78, 141; coup of, 60–64; regime of, 6, 64–79, 105, 110

Marxist Circle, 27, 28–29, 38, 43, 45, 140, 141, 143
media, 17, 19, 44, 69; censorship, 39, 45; under Pol Pot, 113–117; propaganda, 102–103, 115, 116

Norodom Sihanouk, 22–25, 27, 29, 31–32, 35, 37, 38–39, 105, 141, 142; "democratic" rule of, 40–43, 44–45, 47–49, 51, 53–55, 56–57; in exile, 63–64, 66, 77; loses control, 57–58, 60–63; after Pol Pot, 131–132, 133, 136; under Pol Pot, 95, 117, 126, 127
Nuon Chea, 76, 95, 96, 118, 132, 137, 139, 142

Phnom Penh, 15, 17, 50, 71, 72–73, 76–79, 93, 94, 110, 114, 128; evacuation of, 8, 78, 83–84, 93; Vietnam takes, 126–127
Pol Pot (Saloth Sar), 8, 142–143; childhood, 11–13, 142; becomes Communist, 27, 28–29, 33, 142; death, 137–139, 143; education, 10, 16, 18, 21–22, 26–29; in exile, 129–130, 132; heads Khmer Rouge, 8, 42–43, 48, 64, 76, 95, 117, 135, 137–138; ideals of, 28, 80–81, 94, 99–100, 119, 138; marriages, 44, 132; names of, 21, 95, 142–143; purges, 95–98, 103–105, 118, 121, 138; resignation, 131, 134–135; trial of, 138

refugees, 6, 71, 73, 103–104, 108, 130–131, 135; organize resistance, 124–127
religion, 14, 92, 94, 107, 129, 132; Buddhism, 15, 16, 17, 19, 20, 30, 69, 94, 134

Saloth Sar. *See* Pol Pot (Saloth Sar)
self-criticism, 106–107, 116–117
social reorganization, 82–86, 88–89, 105, 108–110
Son Ngoc Thanh, 17–18, 19, 20, 21, 23, 24, 31–32, 33
Son Sen, 43, 48, 67, 68, 96, 103, 118, 132, 137, 138, 143
Soviet Union, 10, 12–13, 27, 28, 35, 51, 59, 62, 120, 128, 133

Ta Mok, 98, 103, 118, 121, 132, 137–138, 143
torture, 92, 93, 98, 103, 104, 118

United Nations (UN), 24, 123, 127, 129–130, 131, 132, 134, 135–136
United States, 27, 34, 35, 38; and Cambodia, 39, 41, 46, 49, 51, 56–57, 60, 63, 64–65, 68, 77; and Khmer Rouge, 86–87, 120–121, 123, 128, 135, 137, 139; and Vietnam, 38–39, 49–50, 56, 64, 127–128, 133
urban evacuations, 6–8, 82, 83–84

Vietnam, 10–11, 24, 30, 35–36; in Cambodia, 14, 65, 101–102, 123–134, 141, 142, 143; Pol Pot and, 10–11, 100–102, 104, 120–122, 123, 133; withdraws from Cambodia, 133–136
Vietnam War, 10–11, 36, 38, 46, 49–51, 56, 63, 72, 86; in Cambodia, 10–11, 56–57, 64–68, 72; First Indochinese War, 24–25, 34, 35–36

PHOTO ACKNOWLEDGMENTS

The images in this book are used with the permission of: AP Photo/Kyodo News, p. 1; © Claude Juvenal/AFP/Getty Images, pp. 7, 81, 91; © Laura Westlund/Independent Picture Service, p. 9; © Shirley Hu/Dreamstime.com, p. 14; © AFP/Getty Images, pp. 25, 84, 111, 121; © Howard Sochurek/Time Life Pictures/Getty Images, pp. 32, 39; AP Photo, pp. 36, 50, 62; AP Photo/Max Nash, p. 53; © Tim Page/CORBIS, p. 57; © Larry Burrows/Time Life Pictures/Getty Images, p. 66; Documentation Center of Cambodia, p. 70; © Christine Spengler/Sygma/CORBIS, p. 73; © Patrick Chauvel/Sygma/CORBIS, p. 75; © US Navy/Time Life Pictures/Getty Images, p. 87; © UPPA/Photoshot, p. 92; © Sygma/CORBIS, p. 96; © Richard Dudman/Sygma/CORBIS, p. 102; © Tuol Sleng Museum of Genocide, pp. 104, 107, 115, 122; © John Bryson/Time Life Pictures/Getty Images, p. 125; © Bettmann/CORBIS, p. 127; © Jose Azel/Aurora/Getty Images, p. 130; © David A. Harvey/National Geographic/Getty Images, p. 136; © Prasit Sangrungrueng/AFP/Getty Images, p. 138.

Front cover: © Lyndon Giffard/Alamy (top); © Jehangir Gazdar/ Woodfin Camp/Time Life Images/Getty Images, (bottom).

AUTHOR BIOGRAPHY

Matthew S. Weltig began his career studying eastern Asia. He later taught there for several years and then returned to the United States to study and teach language as a university lecturer. Weltig works in the field of language testing and learning. He also writes on topics in world history. He lives with his wife, Yan, in Monterey, California.